Stevie Smith

Twayne's English Authors Series

Kinley E. Roby, Editor
Northeastern University

TEAS 472

STEVIE SMITH
Photograph courtesy of James MacGibbon.

Stevie Smith

By Sanford Sternlicht

Syracuse University

Twayne Publishers
A Division of G.K. Hall & Co. • Boston

Stevie Smith
Sanford Sternlicht

Copyright 1990 by G. K. Hall & Co.
All rights reserved.
Published by Twayne Publishers
A Division of G. K. Hall & Co.
70 Lincoln Street
Boston, Massachusetts 02111

Excerpts from Stevie Smith: *The Collected Poems of Stevie Smith.*
© 1972 by Stevie Smith. Reprinted by permission of New
Directions Publishing Corporation.

Copyediting supervised by Barbara Sutton
Book production by Gabrielle B. McDonald
Book design by Barbara Anderson

Typeset in 11 pt. Garamond
by Compositors Corporation, Cedar Rapids, Iowa

Printed on permanent/durable acid-free paper
and bound in the United States of America

First published, 1990.
10 9 8 7 6 5 4 3 2 1

Library of Congress Cataloging-in-Publication Data

Sternlicht, Sanford V.
      Stevie Smith / by Sanford Sternlicht.
          p.   cm. — (Twayne's English authors series ; TEAS 472)
      Includes bibliographical references.
      ISBN 0-8057-6990-0 (alk. paper)
      1. Smith, Stevie, 1902–1971—Criticism and interpretation.
   I. Title.   II. Series.
   PR6037.M43Z875   1990
   828'.91209—dc20   89-39236
                                                            CIP

Contents

About the Author

Sanford Sternlicht, professor emeritus of theater and English at the State University of New York at Oswego, is currently adjunct professor of English at Syracuse University. He is the author of the following books: *Gull's Way* (1961), poetry; *Love in Pompeii* (1967), poetry; *The Black Devil of the Bayous* (1970), history, with E. M. Jameson; *John Webster's Imagery and the Webster Canon* (1972); *McKinley's Bulldog: The Battleship Oregon* (1977), history; *John Masefield* (1977); *C. S. Forester* (1981); *USF Constellation: Yankee Racehorse* (1981), history, with E. M. Jameson; *Padraic Colum* (1985); *John Galsworthy* (1987); and *R. F. Delderfield* (1988).

He has edited *Selected Short Stories of Padraic Colum* (1985), *Selected Plays of Padraic Colum* (1986), and *Selected Poems of Padraic Colum* (1989). His many articles on subjects from Shakespeare to Graham Greene have appeared in numerous journals, and his poetry has appeared in over three hundred publications. He received the *Writer Magazine* New Poets Award in 1960 and a poetry fellowship from the Poetry Society of America in 1965.

Preface

The art of Stevie Smith is an idiosyncratic one. In a macabre, satirical way this cult poet, who worked over thirty years as a secretary and lived all but the first three years of her life in the same suburban London house, constructed a lyrical metaphysic based on the inexhaustable theme of death and oblivion. She is to poetry what Edvard Munch is to painting; she is the poet of frozen anguish. Her curious, cruelly comic verse rushed out of a tortured mouth that somehow managed to laugh. If our history is not only what we do, but also what we imagine, desire, or regret, then Stevie Smith's life, more so than many modern poets, is fully chronicled in her work.

Stevie Smith was, simultaneously, a wounded she-devil savaging male privilege and a gay, witty woman enjoying her gender role in a patriarchal society while spoofing it. At the height of her popularity she mounted the reader's platform and sang her Crazy Jane poems in an off-key voice, looking like a middle-aged Lolita. This unlikely candidate for culthood became the subject of a West End London play and a motion picture. Perfecting the short, jabbing poem, Stevie punched her way to a significant and permanent place in twentieth-century English letters.

In her lifetime Stevie Smith earned two separate and distinct reputations: the young avant-garde novelist in the 1930s who also wrote poetry, and the fiercely honest and totally committed poet of the 1950s and 1960s. It is as the latter that Stevie will be remembered.

The purpose of this book is to evaluate the canon of Stevie Smith's work and to attempt to account for its continuing popularity. Also, the major themes of Stevie's work are here delineated and explicated, while homage is paid to her fine seriocomic ear, her Thurberesque zaniness, and her profound ability both to verbalize and symbolize the melancholy, the frustration, the rage, and the vengefulness of the intelligent women of her generation.

The present book is the first all-encompassing study of Stevie Smith's multi-faceted writing, for the first time giving full attention to her novels and short stories, and scrutinizing and assaying the total canon. All previous studies of Stevie's poetry have been thematic in approach; yet Stevie was an artist with several voices that altered as time went by, and this study documents this growth by proceeding along developmental lines. Another original contribution of this book is the critical evaluation of the previously uncollected and mostly unavailable short fiction and the uncollected poems of Stevie Smith recently published in *Me Again*.

I have chosen to call Stevie Smith "Stevie" in this book not out of sexist condescension but because she would have preferred the moniker. Florence Margaret Smith reveled in the autonomy and the illusion of male freedom her nickname initially gave her. As a celebrity in later years it was an appropriate sobriquet. Thus "Stevie" works better than "Smith," as "Satchmo" works better than "Armstrong," "Marilyn" better than "Monroe" or "Baker," and "Dylan" better than "Zimmerman." Anyway, her friends and the readers who relish her work did and do merely call her Stevie.

I take this opportunity to thank James MacGibbon, literary executor of the estate of Stevie Smith, and New Directions Publishing Corp. for kind permission to publish from the poetry and drawings of Stevie Smith (*The Collected Poems of Stevie Smith*, © 1972).

It would be remiss of me here not to thank the scholars Jack Barbera and William McBrien for their ground-breaking work as biographers, editors, and bibliographers of Stevie Smith and her work. Also to be thanked are Dr. Wendy Bousfield, William D. West, Joanne Jones, Mary Ellen O'Connell, and the interlibrary loan staff of Bird Library, Syracuse University.

Sanford Sternlicht

Syracuse University

Chronology

1902   Florence Margaret Smith born 20 September in Hull, Yorkshire. Second daughter of Ethel Spear Smith and Charles Ward Smith.

1906   Father deserts family. Mother, aunt Margaret, sister Molly, and Stevie move to London suburb of Palmers Green where Stevie lives for the rest of her life.

1907   Enrolled in private school: the Palmers Green High School and Kindergarten. Contracts tubercular peritonitis and for three years schooling alternates with residence in Yarrow Convalescent Home, Broadstairs, on the Kent coast.

1917   Enrolled in North London Collegiate School for Girls.

1919   Mother dies.

1920   Takes six-month course at Mrs. Hoster's Secretarial Training College. Father remarries.

1922   Nicknamed "Stevie."

1923   Commences thirty-year career as secretary with publishing firm of C. Arthur Pearson, Ltd., later called Newnes, Pearson, Ltd. Sister leaves home.

1924   Begins writing poems.

1929   First holiday in Germany.

1931   Second holiday in Germany. Tours with Karl Eckinger, first lover.

1932   Relationship with Eric Armitage, second lover.

1935   Finally in print with acceptances of six poems by *New Statesman*.

1936   *Novel on Yellow Paper.*

1937   *A Good Time Was Had by All.*

1938   *Over the Frontier. Tender Only to One.*

1939   Begins wartime volunteer service as a nighttime air-raid fire watcher.

1942   Brief relationship with George Orwell. *Mother, What Is Man?*

1949   Father dies. *The Holiday.*

1950   *Harold's Leap.*

1953   Attempts suicide. Is retired with pension from Newnes, Pearson. Begins years of heavy book reviewing.

1957   *Not Waving but Drowning.*

1958   *Some Are More Human than Others: Sketchbook.*

1959   Radio play *A Turn Outside* produced by the BBC.

1961   Undergoes surgery for removal of arthritic knee cap.

1962   *Selected Poems.*

1966   Cholmondeley Award for Poetry. *The Frog Prince and Other Poems. Penguin Modern Poets 8.*

1968   Aunt Margaret dies at age ninety-six.

1969   Awarded the Gold Medal for Poetry by Queen Elizabeth II. *The Best Beast.*

1971   Dies from an inoperable brain tumor on 7 March.

1972   *Scorpion and Other Poems.*

1975   *Collected Poems.*

1977   *Stevie: A Play from the Life and Work of Stevie Smith* by Hugh Whitemore, produced in London.

1978   *Stevie,* motion picture starring Glenda Jackson, released.

1981   *Me Again: Uncollected Writings of Stevie Smith.*

Chapter One
The Physical Thing

In the 1960s Stevie Smith was a British celebrity, a platform poet, a popular reciter who caught the attention of the hippie generation. Her agnosticism, her fascination with death and oblivion, and her perspective on love, war, aggression, and male power made her a cult figure among radical, educated youth. Her audience loved the small, pale, hunched, middle-aged woman with a fringe of straight hair clipped across her forehead and a mobile face usually sporting a quizzical expression, like a little girl recoiling from too loud a noise.

In fact Stevie Smith was a conservative, reclusive, somewhat miserly, suburban middle-class woman, as much a Tory as any stuffy club man. She could be as hidebound a Victorian as her old aunt, whom she called "the Lion Aunt," and with whom she lived for sixty-two years, while, paradoxically, she craved the company of writers and exulted in the belated public recognition she received in the last decade of her life.

Much more importantly, however, Stevie was a hard-working poet with an original style and a fierce commitment to artistic truth. She thought that "a poet should get on with his work and not be bothered by what his status is in the community."[1] Furthermore, Stevie believed that she had a significant place in contemporary British poetry. "The times will just have to enlarge themselves to make room for me, won't they?" she said.[2]

Childhood

Stevie Smith was born Florence Margaret Smith on 20 September 1902 in Hull, Yorkshire, forty-two days after the coronation of Edward VII. She was the daughter of Ethel Spear Smith and Charles Ward Smith. Her only sibling, Molly, had been born on 24 January 1901.

The daughter of a successful civil engineer, Ethel Spear Smith was a frail romantic who married a handsome, curly-haired man with a taste for drink and wanderlust. Charles Ward Smith had a boyhood dream of becoming a naval officer, but after his two elder brothers drowned, his mother refused his request to attend the Royal Naval College at Osborne, and Charles was placed in the family coal-exporting business as a forwarding agent. He continued to dream of the sea even when at the age of twenty-six he married the beautiful Ethel Spear on 1 September 1898. The next year the Boer War broke out and Charles wanted to join up, but Ethel was pregnant.

Neither Molly nor "Peggy" were well children. Peggy, born two months premature, almost did not survive. Her father was in Ostend on business at the time of her birth. His trips away from home grew longer and longer. Finally, in 1906, the thirty-four-year-old Charles Smith ran to his dream; he abandoned a wife with a weak heart, two sickly daughters, and a neglected family business, for a life at sea with the White Star Line. The Smiths never divorced. Ethel continued to think of herself as married to Charles, but he did not return home except for a rare visit, and he did not support his family financially. Parenting, for him, consisted of sending picture postcards from exotic ports. During World War I he achieved his boyhood desire and became a naval officer serving on the antisubmarine North Sea Patrol.

When Charles Smith abandoned his family, Ethel Smith could no longer afford the home at 34 De La Pole Avenue, Hull, in which the children had been born.[3] Ethel Smith and her unmarried sister, Margaret Annie Spear, using their modest inheritance, moved to London with the girls in the autumn of 1906, where educational opportunities for the children would be better, setting up what Stevie later called "a house of female habitation."[4] The women occupied a semidetached red brick terrace house, 1 Avondale Road, in the suburb of Palmers Green, eight miles from the heart of the capital.[5] It was Stevie's address for the rest of her life. The family barely survived on the interest from Grandfather Spear's legacy. Stevie nursed a lifelong resentment against her father. She took the desertion personally, and it made her suspicious of men and their commitments.

Education

Stevie's Edwardian childhood was not idyllic, and it was not because of a lack of money. Her mother and her aunt managed to send her to a pleasant, competent, private elementary school, the Palmers Green High School and Kindergarten, three streets from home. When still only five years old, however, she fell ill with tubercular peritonitis and was sent to the Yarrow Convalescent Home at Broadstairs on the Kent coast, where she resided on and off for three years. Stevie was never completely healthy from then on and, despite the family's attempt to fatten her up somewhat with milk and eggs, remained a very thin woman until middle age.

Stevie's ten years in Palmers Green High School and Kindergarten produced a capable if not brilliant student. The family became communicants in the Anglican Church of St. John the Evangelist. Stevie retained that affiliation even though she later considered herself an "Anglican agnostic," as far as such a thing is possible. From childhood on it was the hymns she loved and the thought that God, existing or not, made humankind less lonely in the universe. The church did, however, provide intellectual and cultural activities in the form of lectures, lantern slide shows, and amateur theatricals; and it subtly furnished the basis for her theology and her metaphysical poetic in the time to come.

Mrs. Smith's health continued to decline. Soon she needed a wheelchair to get about. World War I and the ensuing zeppelin raids on London were hard on the nervous inhabitants of 1 Avondale Road. The girls at Palmers Green High ducked under blankets draped over desks for protection during air raids and drills.[6] Like so many Londoners, Stevie would endure the fury of aerial bombardment again in World War II.

Stevie concluded her years at Palmers Green High in July 1917, receiving a prize for literature but no scholarship for further study at her next school, the North London Collegiate School for Girls in Camden Town. Molly had won a scholarship, and Mrs. Smith wanted the girls in the same school. Stevie was not an outstanding scholar at North London Collegiate. She won only a single prize, and that was for scripture. Her voice was not good, though she could sing loudly enough, and she was asked not to join in the songs. Her voice improved little with time.

In March 1918 Stevie was confirmed in the church in which she had been baptized as an infant. On 12 January 1919 Mrs. Smith fell gravely ill with congestive heart failure. Her extremities became gangrenous. Mr. Smith was notified, and on 6 February he arrived in time to see his wife die. Charles Smith made a powerful show of grief at the funeral, and he visited his children several times prior to his demobilization from the Royal Navy in December 1919, but only a few months later he married a woman fifteen years his junior and took up poultry farming. Stevie could never bring herself to visit him.[7]

Meanwhile Stevie passed her matriculation exams. She left North London Collegiate, and, as she was not considered university material, she enrolled in Mrs. Hoster's Secretarial Training College in central London for a six-month course.[8] She was bored by it, but secretarial work was one of the few skilled jobs open to women at the time.

In 1920 Stevie received her nickname, although she would always be Peggy to her aunt Margaret. In truth, she led a double life beginning in the 1930s. In her Palmers Green world she was Peggy or Florence Margaret, but in the literary world of inner London she became Stevie. The sobriquet came from a horseback-riding incident. While riding on one of the London commons with a male friend, she spurred her mount gently but not too successfully and some little boys shouted sarcastically, "Come on Steve," referring to Steve Donaghue, a popular jockey of the day. Her friend started to call her Steve, too, alluding to her jockey size. Other friends altered it to "Stevie."[9] It caught on. Stevie grew to love the distinction, the anonymity, and the androgynous freedom the name gave her.

Working

After finishing with Mrs. Hoster's, Stevie got a job in the office of a consulting engineer. After a year she obtained the position she would hold for the remainder of her working days: in 1923 she became private secretary to Sir Neville Pearson, chairman of the publishing firm of C. Arthur Pearson, Ltd., later called Newnes, Pearson, Ltd. (Sir Neville was the model for Sir Phoebus Ullwater, Bt., in *Novel on Yellow Paper* [1936].) Stevie's secretarial job at Pearson's was neither physically nor mentally taxing. She found time to write poems while at work. It was nearly eleven years before any of the poems were published, but the effort had begun.

Stevie's great aunt, Martha Hearn Clode, who had been living with Stevie and Aunt Margaret from 1916 on, died in 1924 at age eighty-four. At this time Molly was a university graduate teaching in Suffolk, so Stevie and the Lion Aunt, whom she loved dearly, were now alone. For the next forty-four years they lived happily together. Aunt Margaret was the great love of Stevie's life, a mother, sister, and, in the sense of nurturer and homemaker, wife to Stevie as long as the older woman had strength to serve. When Miss Spear became an invalid and was confined to the second floor of the house, Stevie moved her life upstairs to cook and clean and care for the woman who had done the same for her for so many years.

An event that affected Stevie's development as a writer was Molly's conversion to Roman Catholicism in 1928. Stevie and her aunt were disturbed by this breach of family unity. Stevie, particularly, was very concerned with harmonization in the church whose dignity and ceremony she loved. For her the Anglican church mitigated more successfully than other Christian churches what Stevie saw as the cruelties of Christianity. Even though they were never openly hostile to each other, Stevie and her sister for many years refought the English Reformation. Neither sister even tergiversated, although the death of their aunt and Molly's failing health brought a truce late in their lives. Still, the controversy helped to keep Stevie thinking about religion, and it helped formulate her metaphysics.

Additionally, Molly's academic success caused Stevie to feel somewhat disgraced over her own lack of a university degree. It was as if office work was her punishment for not having studied harder and performed better in school. So early on Stevie began a lifelong regimen of reading the classics. What she purposely did not read was contemporary poetry. She was convinced that "one will get the lines crossed and begin writing their poems."[10] Instead she read and studied the romantic poets, Mary Shelley, the novels of D. H. Lawrence and Aldous Huxley, French criticism, Oscar Wilde, Virginia Woolf, Franz Kafka, and the *Ethics* of Spinoza.[11] Her eclectic reading was pursued voraciously. She read a new book every day or two. Her incessant speed-reading helped her later on to earn part of her livelihood as a book reviewer.

Love

In 1929 and 1931 Stevie spent two week-long holidays in Germany. The first was pleasant and relatively uneventful. On the second, while staying with Jewish friends in Berlin, she saw a swastika scrawled on their gatepost and began to see, think about, and understand the dark and ominous side of the German character. More significant for her personal life, however, was her chance meeting in the National Gallery with Karl Eckinger, a Swiss-German graduate student in history whose acquaintance she had made previously in London. A romance ensued in Germany and in England.

Karl was six feet two inches tall, blue eyed, two years younger than Stevie, and very formal.[12] He wore glasses and presented a calling card stating: "Karl Eckinger, stud. phil." Stevie saved his card the rest of her life. Karl's constant, nationalistic harping on the superiority of things German, as the Nazis were rising to power, destroyed the relationship. After idyllic trysts in the English countryside they parted ways as completely and as swiftly as England and Germany parted ways in the darkening days before World War II. At least one of Stevie's friends at the time considered Karl a Nazi and believed that Stevie, partly under Karl's influence, was anti-Semitic then.[13] It seems more likely that Stevie shared the unfortunate prewar trait among many British writers, artists, and intellectuals of snobbery toward Jews, who "weren't really English" and who were "pushy" in social and business matters. That attitude was quickly extirpated as fascist evil became more and more evident. Stevie came to loathe Germany, and her anti-German feelings remained as long as she lived.

Another lover, Eric Armitage, soon entered Stevie's life. They probably
met at a church social in 1932. Eric was a tall, dark-haired, handsome man
with a stammer. There was an informal engagement. Neither party was very
enthusiastic. Stevie soon realized that despite their physical compatibility a
marriage could not succeed. They were too different and she too set in her
ways. He was practical and down to earth and wanted a conventional wife.
Stevie at thirty could not be that sort of person.

Stevie remained fond of men. She was not afraid of sex nor was she a les-
bian, but she never again contemplated a personal commitment with a man.
Sex and intimate male companionship receded in importance in her life. She
said: "I love life, I adore it, but only because I keep myself well on the edge. I
wouldn't commit myself to anything."[14] Although she always had several
male friends, eventually her view of male-female relations would be: "I doubt
for instance if the tomcat is ever satisfied; in the hands of Nature sex is a
tyrant's weapon."[15] As for children: "I'm very fond of children. Why I admire children so much is that I think all the time, ' Thank heaven they aren't
mine.' "[16] It was her aunt whom Stevie loved and trusted. Their domestic life
was enough for both of them. Stevie could always warm her hands at the
hearths of her married friends.

Sudden Fame

In 1934 Stevie made her first attempt at publishing her poetry. She submitted a large collection of her poems to Curtis Brown, Ltd., literary agents.
As is the custom, the collection was given to a reader for assessment, who
found the work an oddly macaronic celebration of ugliness, deplorably snob-
bish in its classical allusions, and of dubious literary quality. The reader also
did not approve of the illustrations Stevie submitted with her poems. Finally,
the next year Stevie got six poems accepted by the writer-critic David
Garnett, then literary editor of the *New Statesman*. Encouraged, Stevie tried
again the same year for book publication of her verse. She made a submission
to Chatto and Windus. A young editor, Ian Parsons, sent her away with in-
struction to write a novel. Stevie dutifully and quickly obliged. Typing at
home and at work on the yellow office paper used at Pearson's for carbon
copies, she finished *Novel on Yellow Paper* in only six weeks.

In February 1936 Chatto and Windus promptly turned the novel down.
To the publisher's reader it seemed too derivative of Laurence Sterne's
Tristram Shandy, too quixotic, not structured enough, and without commer-
cial possibilities.

Undaunted, Stevie sent the manuscript to the publisher Jonathan Cape, who had seen one of Stevie's poems in the *New Statesman* and had requested a manuscript from her. He expected a collection of verse and got a novel, which he liked and published in 1936. By then Stevie had already begun a sequel. Meanwhile, *Novel on Yellow Paper* received widespread and excellent reviews, and Stevie was thrilled by her sudden fame. She was thrust out of the world of Pearson's and Palmers Green into the inner circles of the London literary scene. One reviewer in 1938 noted: "During the last eighteen months or so, there has been no more striking feature of English letters than the rise and sudden arrival of Miss Stevie Smith."[17] All her life Stevie loved publishers's parties and luncheons with fellow authors.[18]

Happy with the success of *Novel on Yellow Paper*, Cape accepted and published in 1937 Stevie's first book of poetry, *A Good Time Was Had by All*, with her illustrations. Containing the best of ten years of Stevie's efforts, it too was received exceptionally well, especially for a first book of poetry. Astute readers recognized that here was a new and distinct voice in British poetry. Without literary or social ties, out of the ambit of the poetry establishment, indeed perhaps without having read much of the work of the Georgian poets or the later moderns like W. H. Auden, Stephen Spender, Louis MacNeice, or Dylan Thomas, Stevie was what she appeared: sui generis. That perception rightly endures. Now it was easy for Stevie to place poems in such leading British periodicals as the *London Mercury, The Bystander,* and *Granta,* as well as the *New Statesman.*

Stevie's second novel, *Over the Frontier,* was published by Jonathan Cape in 1938. Although respectfully received by such review periodicals as the London *Times Literary Supplement,* it was not as successful as *Novel on Yellow Paper.* Many critics and readers were puzzled by the stylistic shift from realism to surrealism in midbook and by a plot that grows more and more fantastical. The *Observer* critic, Frank Swinnerton, had difficulty understanding Stevie's rhetoric. He "did not understand what 'Frontier' [was] crossed in the book," and refused to "grope after hidden meanings."[19]

Stevie's new friends noted that the recently successful thirty-six-year-old author greatly desired, expected, and demanded to be fawned over and doted upon like a precocious child. She wanted to be spoiled. She began to dress in clothes that were suggestive of a schoolgirl's, and she sometimes did mischievous things and used baby talk. Of course her infantilism also reflected a perspective on life and art that manifested itself in the deceptively ingenuous quality of much of her poetry, but it also surely was a nervous reaction to her newfound and completely unexpected celebrity. It was as if Stevie were saying: "It is only because I am a clever child that I have received this approval, not because I am a mature artist." Additionally,

Stevie's odd actions and dress may have been manifestations of an unconscious cry for help and comfort on the part of a person who had been "abandoned" as a child by father and mother.

Politics

Several of Stevie's new literary acquaintances were part of the literary Left. She was continually introduced to communist writers, particularly those affiliated with Cambridge University, but remained staunchly conservative in her politics. She spoke out against communists and fellow travelers in both pre–World War II and cold war days. Her seemingly inherited Church of England and Tory party positions were unshakable.

In June 1937 Stevie sent the manuscript of a third novel "Married to Death," to her friend and discover David Garnett. After reading the draft, he sent her a letter that was painful both for him to write and for Stevie to read. He could not finish the novel. It was without structure and much too personal. Her autobiographical heroine from *Novel on Yellow Paper* and *Over the Frontier,* Pompey Casmilus, needed replacing. Stevie had to branch out if she was to continue to write long fiction. She abandoned "Married to Death."

However, Jonathan Cape published a second volume of verse, *Tender Only to One,* in November 1938. Writing approvingly in the *New Statesman,* George Stonier noted that Stevie's "writing has the air of an odd, only, lonely child. . . . [*Tender Only to One*] is a mixture of nostalgia and parody, of poetry and jingle."[20]

Wartime

In *Over the Frontier* Stevie presented a prophetic portrait of women as soldiers. As war approached, thousands of women began to don uniforms to serve in the armed forces. Stevie attended first-aid and gas-attack lectures, and when hostilities commenced she became an air-raid warden and fire watcher in the city. During the London blitz she worked in the publishing house all day, returned home via the Piccadilly line underground, walked to Avondale Road, ate with her aunt, and took the tube back to central London to fire-watch much of the night, staying all night in the West End building she was guarding. Meanwhile, Stevie had joined PEN, the international writers' organization, because it was helping to bring refugee authors and editors out of both occupied and soon-to-be-occupied Europe.

Stevie's secretarial salary did not keep up with the inflation caused by the military buildup. Her income from writing was always modest. Pinched, she began an additional career as a book reviewer. Her reviews were renowned for their incisiveness and acumen. Stevie also tried to obtain a position with the British Broadcasting Corporation, but her self-serving boss, Sir Neville Pearson, discouraged her, convincing his valuable secretary that her voice was not clear and that she lisped.[21]

During this period Stevie grew closer through correspondence to her friend from the mid-1930s, the novelist Oliva Manning, at whose wedding she had been a bridesmaid, and whom she had sent to Jonathan Cape with her first novel. Manning was in Bucharest with her husband, who was working for the British Council. Stevie kept her informed of London happenings while Manning was in the Balkans, Egypt, and the Middle East. However, the two writers enjoyed gossip and intrigue too much for the good of their relationship, which remained a troubled one throughout Stevie's life. In 1971, as Stevie lay on her death bed, Oliva Manning was apprised of Stevie's fatal illness. She replied: "Well, if she's really dying, send her my love." Told of her "friend's" remark, the dying Stevie laughed.[22]

Besides working at her office job, fire-watching, reviewing books, and trying to survive in a city that was systematically being reduced to rubble, Stevie also wrote what would be her final novel, *The Holiday*. It was hard, grueling work for Stevie, whose heart was not in it. The novel underwent much revision and rewriting before it finally saw print in 1949. While working on *The Holiday* and during World War II, Stevie became close to the novelist George Orwell, whose later novels *Animal Farm* (1945) and *Nineteen Eighty-Four* (1949) reflect a conservative, anticommunist political view shared by Stevie. Orwell worked at Bush House, BBC Headquarters. Stevie was trying to make inroads there. Some of Stevie's friends believed that she and Orwell had an affair, and Stevie was quoted as saying: "I was living with George Orwell and it wasn't easy."[23] Orwell was married at the time and Stevie was with her aunt, so "living together" must be taken figuratively. Later, Stevie became very angry with Orwell because he denied her the opportunity to broadcast her poetry and prose on the Overseas Program, which he controlled, but her strong feelings may have been due partially to his ending their affair.

In the later war years, Stevie began to have difficulty placing poems in periodicals. Magazines and journals were cutting down on the size and number of pages to conserve paper. Also, Stevie's work seemed frivolous to some, given the grave events of the day. In 1940 she was unsuccessful in convincing her publisher to bring out another volume of her poetry. Finally and reluctantly, Jonathan Cape relented, and *Mother, What Is Man?* came out in 1942.

Stevie made another important lifelong friend during the war years. Kay Dick, the novelist, was then an editor of *John O'London's Weekly*. Their friendship endured to Stevie's death. One result of it was Dick's book of conversations and reflections: *Ivy & Stevie: Ivy Compton-Burnett and Stevie Smith* (1971).

Postwar Years

In 1945, as World War II came to an end, Stevie finished what she thought would be the final version of *The Holiday*.[24] It was not satisfactory to her publisher, so Stevie rewrote it, shifting its time period to the late 1940s. She was also busy writing and publishing short stories during the postwar period, some of them so acrimoniously personal in description that they cost her friendships. *The Holiday* was finally accepted, after several rejections, by the publishers Chapman and Hall, and it came out in 1949.

In the postwar period Stevie also began to give public readings of her poetry. She did so for the money, which she needed badly, and for the satisfaction of the growing recognition it provided her. More and more she began to chant her poems in an off-pitch voice, using English folk tunes and hymns for the near-melodies.

On 20 February 1949 Charles Ward Smith died in the District General Hospital, Kidderminster, Worcestershire. His second wife had died earlier, and he named his daughters executors of his estate. Stevie was too busy to attend his funeral. She was preparing to read a story on the BBC, and it was more important to her to impress and break in with the broadcasting power than to take time to pay respects to a man she never respected.

Fading Popularity

In the 1950s Stevie's poetry clearly went out of fashion. Chapman and Hall were not eager to publish another volume of her verse. *Harold's Leap* was published in the autumn of 1950 but it sold poorly even for a book of verse.

Stevie's greatest need was to get free of her stifling office job. She considered editing. Besides being more interesting, it could also earn her more money. However, she felt the competition was fierce. In 1949 she wrote: "A girl who might be happy as a secretary where the gentler qualities are in demand . . . might be very unhappy in an editor's job which means being on your toes all the time and keeping ahead of the rival ladies who edit other magazines."[25]

Trying to work as a creative writer and holding down a full-time secretarial job, as well as taking increasing care of the Lion Aunt, who was approaching eighty, was extremely enervating and exhausting for Stevie, who was always high strung and never robust. The tension, the frustration, and the wrongs all came to a head for Stevie in 1953. Poems were being rejected regularly. Chapman and Hall had refused to publish another collection of her poetry, citing poor sales of *Harold's Leap* as the reason. She felt that in a conspiritorial way she was being locked out of the poetry scene. In April she wrote her most famous poem, "Not Waving but Drowning," a despair-filled piece of black humor. She was affected by a painful knee condition. She had been disputing with the Inland Revenue. She thought of herself as a servant, not as an independent person. On 1 July 1953 Stevie slashed her wrists in her office. After medical treatment she was taken home to recuperate and rest. Her physician reported to her employer, Sir Neville Pearson, that she was not emotionally or physically able to go back to work, and so at the age of fifty-one Stevie was retired. Her pension was not exceedingly generous, and Stevie had to supplement it with constant reviewing of almost any book sent to her. As her poems were not being published, she slipped an occasional one into a review.

Full-time Writer

Despite the paucity of funds, Stevie now at last could write full-time and be free to travel and visit friends. Stevie worked hard to get yet another volume of poetry in print. Publishing houses, however, were either unwilling to risk money on a volume of her poems, or they refused to publish her drawings with the poems, a condition Stevie insisted upon. After vacillating, the house of André Deutsch brought out Stevie's fifth volume of verse, *Not Waving but Drowning*, in 1957.

Stevie always fought desperately to have her drawings included with her poetry, not because she considered herself to be an accomplished visual artist, but because she had come to feel that the drawings were parts of the poems, rather as introductions, explications, or commentaries. *Not Waving but Drowning* received more critical attention than had *Harold's Leap*. It was all favorable. Critics were fascinated by the funny-peculiar manner of her work in the new collection. Essentially, the critical world was looking at the poetry of Stevie Smith with a fresh perspective. It was a matter of timing. The French theater of the absurd was coming into vogue, and Stevie's work fit in with developing literary theory and practice. In 1958 Stevie found a publisher, Gaberbocchus, willing to bring out a book of her captioned drawings, the Thurberesque *Some Are More Human Than Others.*

Famous Again

In the late 1950s and early 1960s Stevie and her work began to appear more and more frequently on BBC radio. In 1958 she made several appearances on a program called "Brain Trust," which answered listeners' questions and discussed current intellectual, political, and social questions. The next year the BBC produced her radio play *A Turn Outside.* Radio exposure increased Stevie's public recognition, which had as much to do with her distinctive voice and personality as her literary abilities.

Even more significantly, this renewed interest was a product of changing critical values and popular taste. New Criticism, which advocated objectivism and valued the well-wrought poem primarily as a set of intrinsic relationships solving aesthetic problems, was being replaced by more phenomenological views in which the poem, in the romantic mode, is returned to the author as a manifestation of his or her consciousness.

In 1959 Stevie introduced and humorously captioned *Cats in Color,* a picture book appreciated by both cat lovers and Stevie Smith fans. Stevie's introduction reminds the reader of T. S. Eliot's *Old Possum's Book of Practical Cats,* although it is evident that Eliot was more of a cherisher of cats than Stevie, who nonetheless once had a feline named Tizdal. Her cats are "nervous creatures," and "we have given them reason to be, not only by our cruelty but our love too, that presses upon them" (*CC*, 9–12). Cats are like children, more interesting when observed, and most adorable when they are someone else's, as Stevie would say.

The year 1960 was physically painful for Stevie. An arthritic knee that she had damaged in school while playing field hockey caused her great pain. A medical specialist recommended surgery, but Stevie initially declined. Finally, unable to cope with the pain and her growing debility, in January 1961 she consented to an operation in which her right kneecap was removed. She remained in the Wood Green and Southgate Hospital until February and then went to Buckinghamshire to recuperate further at the home of a friend, but the pain came back. Eventually she recovered most of the use of her right leg. In October she was back in the hospital again being operated on for a breast tumor that fortunately proved benign.[26]

Stevie's home life with her elderly aunt, who was immobilized by an arthritic hip, was led essentially on the second floor of the house. When Stevie did get out it was generally to read her poetry at a university or at a poetry meeting or for the BBC. She now became a subject herself for BBC radio programming. More and more, the world was seeking her. Poets such as Philip Larkin, Robert Lowell, Thomas Merton, Muriel Rukeyser, and Sylvia Plath praised her work and wanted to meet her. Ogden Nash wrote a poem about Stevie in which he asked:

> Who and what is Stevie Smith?
> Is she women? Is she myth?
> . . . .
> Slipping from her secret nook
> Like a goblin or a spook,
> Searching out her God to haunt him,
> Now to praise him, now to taunt him,
> Then to sing at Man's expense
> Songs of deadly innocence.[27]

Selected Poems, published in 1962, was greeted with great critical acclaim. It and Stevie's inclusion in *Penguin Modern Poets 8* (1966) placed her among the forefront of contemporary English poets. Full American recognition came simultaneously, and soon her poems were being translated into French and German. Reviews of *Selected Poems* compared Stevie to William Blake, Emily Dickinson, and Edward Lear. The wisest critics saw her as a unique voice. One surmised that the animus behind her was "a witch."[28] Stevie rather encouraged the witch imagery. If some men wanted to see her numen as preternatural, why let them; it was good publicity. In writing her own blurb for the American edition of *Selected Poems* (1964), pretending to be another writer, she said of herself: "She is certainly funny. But it is not a humor one would care to meet on a dark night."

Now Stevie's poems appeared in the *New Yorker, Atlantic Monthly, New York Review of Books,* and other leading American periodicals. An attempt was made to bring Stevie to the States for a poetry tour, but she declined. Although she took short holidays in Great Britain and on the Continent, Stevie did not wish to leave the care of her aunt to others too often or for too long, and she really enjoyed traveling best when she was the pampered guest of friends. The thought of an arduous American tour was really too much for Stevie, now well into her sixties, but she pretended that she feared to disappoint her American readers who might mistake her for her sketch of a young girl on the dust jacket of the American edition of *Selected Poems.*[29] Clearly, however, Stevie's energy was diminishing.

Nineteen sixty-six was a great year for Stevie. She won the Cholmondeley

Award for Poetry, and even the Lion Aunt was impressed. Previously, her aunt's comments on Stevie's writing ran to: "I'm very glad to hear you've got another book coming out, but as you know I don't know much about it. It's all nonsense to me, dear." But when Stevie received the award she said: "I wish your mother was alive and could have known about this, dear."[30] It was her highest praise.

The same year another book of poetry, *The Frog Prince and Other Poems,* was brought out by Longmans, Green. It contains seventy-two pieces that had not appeared in book form, plus many reprints of earlier poems. One discerning critic called Stevie "the most original poet writing in English today. . . . She hides nothing, submits herself to a complete exposure which is the hallmark of the great poets."[31]

The Lion Aunt Dies

Stevie's Aunt Margaret died on 11 March 1968 at ninety-six. Stevie was bereft with grief. Her aunt had been a surrogate mother and lifelong companion to her. Margaret Spear was the great, uncritical, warm, and giving love of Stevie's life.

In the same year, Alfred A. Knopf published Stevie's next book of verse in New York. *The Best Beast* contains forty-four poems, some of which, including the title poem, appeared in *The Frog Prince;* others would be reprinted in the posthumous *Scorpion and Other Poems* (1972).

In May 1969 Stevie's sister, Molly, had a stroke, and Stevie temporarily moved down to Molly's bungalow in Buckfast, Devon, in order to help her recover her speech and fight partial paralysis. For many months after Molly left the hospital, Stevie commuted between Palmers Green and Buckfast.

Meeting the Queen

The high point of Stevie's popular recognition came on 21 November 1969 when she received the Gold Medal for Poetry from the hands of Queen Elizabeth II. Typically, Stevie went to a rummage sale at her church to buy a secondhand hat for the occasion. The tiny, nervous parishioner, who dressed like a child in a schoolgirl jumper and a blouse with a Peter Pan collar, who wore her hair in 1920s-style bangs, and from whom the children of Palmers Green ran, shrieking "witch," was going to an audience with the queen.

Stevie tells in a letter how she went alone to Buckingham Palace, arrived too early, bought some picture postcards in the gallery, told a policeman that she had an appointment with the queen, was not believed, and so went for a bit of a walk. When it began to rain she went back to the palace and convinced the guards that she did indeed have an appointment with Her Majesty. She then had a "slightly giggly time with the lady-in-waiting and a very decorative young man" (*MA, 320*). Her audience with the queen lasted twenty minutes. Recounting it in her innocent risible persona Stevie said that she became aware that poetry "wasn't *absolutely* her *very* favourite subject." And when Stevie mentioned that she had been writing about murder recently and began to talk about a recent case, the royal smile "got rather fixed."[32]

The queen's Gold Medal for Poetry was Stevie's last award, but if she had lived longer additional prizes and recognition surely would have accrued. In April 1970 Stevie had a fall in which she cracked three ribs and damaged the knee without the cap (*MA, 321*). Worried unnecessarily about money, she tried to sell some of her manuscripts, and she considered applying for government grants. She feared that further disablement might require extended nursing care for herself in the future. Even though the fees were paltry, as little as fifteen pounds, Stevie gave as many poetry readings as she could physically manage. She was also writing at a fast clip.

In November 1970 Stevie went down to Buckfast to stay with her sister again. She began to lose energy and feel ill. It became very hard for her to meet her reading commitments in the West Country. Soon she had fits of near fainting. She heard ringing in her ears, lost her balance, and began to lose control of her words. Clinical events succeeded each other rapidly. She was soon stammering. Stevie had planned to remain with Molly until just after 1 January and then go on a reading tour that would include Edinburgh and London, but on doctor's orders she canceled.

Conclusion

During the night of 6 January 1971, while still at Molly's, Stevie had great difficulty with her speech and was very sick. She went to Torbay Hospital in Torquay, Devon, where she underwent tests while trying to attend to literary and business affairs. Friends came to visit and saw that she was gravely ill. Her head had been shaved for exploratory surgery and was swathed in a turban of bandages that slipped askew from time to time, revealing gray-pink scalp and grizzled stubble. She was cheerful. She tried to make jokes as her condition deteriorated.

Stevie was taken from Torbay Hospital to Freedom Fields Hospital in Plymouth, and finally to Ashburton Hospital in Ashburton, Devon. She had a malignant, inoperable brain tumor. Stevie was not afraid to die. For her, death was a slave. Her good friend and literary executor James MacGibbon is certain that Stevie tried to signal him to fetch her sleeping pills from home so she could command the slave to do his duty quickly.[33] Stevie Smith died at sixty-eight on 7 March 1971 in Ashburton Hospital. She had not been ill very long and she never became dependent on anyone else. On 12 March a funeral service was held in the Anglican Church of the Holy Trinity in Buckfastleigh, Devon. The body was cremated according to the wishes expressed in her will. Stevie's reputation continued to grow after her death and it has not peaked yet. *Scorpion and Other Poems* was published in 1972. *Stevie: A Play from the Life and Work of Stevie Smith* by Hugh Whitemore was a West End London hit in 1977. A motion picture version of the drama, entitled *Stevie,* was produced in 1978, starring the distinguished actress Glenda Jackson, who had read Stevie's poems publicly, had met the poet, and had admired her.

Born in the Edwardian era, Stevie Smith grew up in a society where girls were reproached for having weaker bodies, brains, determination, endurance, and emotions than boys. If a girl strove to equalize these "handicaps" she was told that she was unfeminine and that no one would love her and marry her. Women were to be an inspiration to the male creative force, helpmates to men. Consciously or unconsciously, Stevie broke out of that trap, not with a powerful, rebellious thrust of a sword, but subversively, with the stealth of oil. Thus she lived her own life. And she found a distinctive voice. Stevie's not drowning but waving.

Chapter Two
The Museum of Everything: The Novels

Stevie Smith's three novels, *Novel on Yellow Paper, Over the Frontier,* and *The Holiday,* are heavily autobiographical. Stevie was a poet by choice, a novelist by need. Like Laurence Sterne's *Tristram Shandy* (1759–67), Stevie's novels are essentially plotless. Nor are they studies in character. The narrator—Pompey Casmilus in *Novel on Yellow Paper* and *Over the Frontier* and Celia in *The Holiday*—is always the protagonist. The narrator sometimes speaks directly to the reader, and at other times, as heroine, she carries on a stream-of-consciousness, interior monologue like Molly Bloom's in James Joyce's *Ulysses* (1922) or the title characters in Virginia Woolf's *Mrs. Dalloway* (1925) and *Orlando* (1928).

The novels of Stevie Smith are elaborate vernacular discussions, intelligent observations, and informed reflections. Their great delight is the verbal ingenuity of the poet-narrator, eclectically alloying archaic language with 1930s American movie slang; Latin, German, French, and Italian with English; and Gothic and fairy-tale devices with short verse—all resulting in a most original style.

Nevertheless, the novels are difficult to read and sometimes exasperating as the reader searches for plot or even description. Despite many brilliant passages—the brassy, Dorothy Parkeresque, "I'm talking to you, pal" prose; surrealistic dream sequences; and erudite discourses on religion, art, education, and politics—the books can seem as dated as the fashions of the period. *Novel on Yellow Paper* especially "elevates self-obsession to the level of a literary device."[1] Furthermore, *Novel on Yellow Paper* and *Over the Frontier* are printed in one piece, without chapter divisions, although time or place changes are implied by doubly indented paragraphs. Only *The Holiday* is divided into regular numbered paragraphs.

Perhaps the greatest achievement of Stevie's novels is that they connect, as few if any contemporary works did, the modern young woman to her world, a place of contradiction where increasing opportunity and continued repression coexist. The novels also link the urban Englishwoman to her mythic,

Anglo-Catholic, and Victorian pasts. And they do so with plangent humor and seeming insouciance.

Novel on Yellow Paper

The voice of Pompey Casmilus speaks to us from the pages of *Novel on Yellow Paper* (1936) like the voice of a flirtatious young woman on an old phonograph record. An intelligent girl experiments, free-associates, vocally mugs, disguises her voice with foreign accents and expressions, teases, plays with words, and switches subjects capriciously, enjoying herself thoroughly in the process as she discourses on almost everything conceivably important to her: love, sex, abortion, marriage, literature, work, religion, suicide, and death.

The plot of *Novel on Yellow Paper,* such as it is, is one that could have been found in a women's magazine like those Stevie's employers published. A young girl who works in an office goes back and forth to work, meets some friends, visits others, falls in love with a man, travels to Germany on holiday, but always returns to her suburban London household where she sojourns with her old aunt. The meetings and visits with friends, whom later she sometimes savages with malice, form the structure of the novel. The heart of the novel's dramatic action is the question of Pompey's marrying or rejecting "dippy" Freddy: "But now I am involved again in love, and I must marry, or I must not marry. . . . I must go, I must come back. Here I am again. Now I am going."[2] Her ambivalence is excruciating. She does not marry. Freddy goes off in a huff. The decision, though a wise one, causes her suffering: "Oh Freddy, how keep you forever at bay? The very words cry out to bring you back. Oh chaps he was sweet was Freddy, there were moods when never sweeter. But oh sweet of sweet, what helps, when sweet in but chimera-coat he trips beside? Now now that will do, do do. Let me have no more of that" (*NYP,* 239).

Pompey calls herself a Dodo and forgoes further self-pity, but it is not easy for her to get Freddy out of her mind, for "Freddy was a great boy for rhyming slang and taught me a lot that time we were in Cornwall that time I rode that high and hungry horse Kismet round the vegetable fields" (*NYP,* 240). Stevie's heroines always ride with their lovers. Riding is a euphemistic metaphor for sex. The abandonment of Freddy means the loss of love and companionship as well as sex with a compatible but too-conventional male. Kismet, the high and hungry horse of fate, symbolizes sexual desire and, assuming the above position, riding and reining the male.

Stevie and Pompey are very hard on women in regard to their sex's relationship with the opposite. Pompey decries the passivity and modest goals of most of their comtemporary sisterhood: "The unmarried girls have an idea, that if only they were married it would be all right, and the married women think, Well now I am married, so it *is* all right: Sometimes too of course it is all right, but sometimes they have to work very hard saying all the time: So now I am married, so now it is all right, so Miss So-and-So is not married, so that is not all right. So what. . . . And the girls who are not married are often getting quite desperate oh yes they are becoming quite desperate" (*NYP,* 149).

Yet even Pompey is ambivalent. She works for a publishing company that keeps women in thralldom by brainwashing them through inane magazine articles into becoming "Good listeners . . . Good Pals. . . . Feminine, they Let him Know they Sew their own Frocks, they sometimes even go so far as to Pay Attention to Personal Hygiene" (*NYP* 151). But then she too waffles in and out of the dominant outlook "that keeps us all kissable" (*NYP* 19).

Stevie is almost as hard on her church, the Church of England, as she is on passive women. She will be harder on it later. Criticizing the church, sometimes caviling, she sums up her position: "But actually I am not a Christian actively. I mean I am actively not a Christian. I have a lot against Christianity though I cannot at the moment remember what it is" (*NYP,* 38).

The name Pompey Casmilus is rooted in things pagan. Like her creator, Pompey has assumed a masculine first name. Pompey the Great was a Roman general, a rival of Julius Caesar. Miss Casmilus is more an image of a decaying classical statue of the general, waiting and passive, although in the sequel, *Over the Frontier,* she will become a soldier. Her name is mythological as well as historical. Casmilus, more correctly Camilus, is another appelation for the Greek god Hermes, the Roman Mercury. Hermes serves others, is often capricious, and is sometimes a liar. He is always a "foot-off-the-ground" fellow as he flies back and forth, and he is a *psychopompos,* who takes dead souls to Hades and always slips out again. Pompey Casmilus is witty, joking, capricious, exaggerating, always traveling, and fascinated with death.

Like an epic poem, *Novel on Yellow Paper* employs iterative imagery as a structural device as well as a thematic vehicle. The major image patterns are those of stone and statuary; emptiness and boredom; classical allusions relating to figures who do fiendish things, like Medea, or suffer strange and horrible ends, like Pentheus; and references to death: "So teach your little ones to look on Death as Thanatos-Hades the great Lord of the Dead, that must, great prince though he be, come to their calling" (*NYP,* 161).

Primarily, *Novel on Yellow Paper* is about unrequited love, a never-meant-to-be love affair gone wrong, heartbreak, controlled hysteria. It is also about loss, sometimes bravely, even stoically faced: what most mortals feel when love dies. The final effect, for all the wit, bravado, and humor, is bleakness. The ambivalence and confusion of twentieth-century woman is evident. Pompey enjoys and is proud of her womanhood, but she also disparages it because she has been conditioned to believe that her gender is the less significant one. To the degree that Pompey devalues her femaleness she estranges herself from her self. That is why Pompey ends her novel with the allegorical dream about the tigress Flo (Stevie's baptismal first name was Florence):

There was pity and incongruity in the death of the tigress Flo. Falling backwards into her pool at Whipsnade she lay there in a fit. The pool was drained and Flo, that mighty and unhappy creature, captured in what jungle darkness for what dishonourable destiny, was subjected to the indignity of artificial respiration.

Yes, chaps, they worked Flo's legs backwards and forwards and sat on Flo's chest. . . . Back came Flo's fled spirit and set her on uncertain pads. She looked, she lurched, and sensing some last, unnameable, not wholly apprehended, final outrage, she fell, she whimpered, clawed in vain, and died. (*NYP,* 252)

Over the Frontier

Over the Frontier (1938) takes up exactly where *Novel on Yellow Paper* leaves off. Pompey is still distraught over the break-up with Freddy. She is using sleeping pills. There is a temporary reconciliation manipulated by Pompey, who despises herself for doing it: "Alas, we do not know whether we are coming or going, whether we should laugh or cry. He is lost, wounded and betrayed by that last old-fashioned hug and kiss under the eddying and unnatural flickering light of these poison green gaslights of the Pentonville Road. So that is what this detestable Pompey has done to her poor Freddy."[3]

The reconciliation fails, however, and Pompey is once more depressed. Despite constant partying she sings of death:

> . . . oh happy night and night's
> companion Death
> What exultation what ecstasy is in thy breath
> It is as salt as the salt silt that lies beneath.
> (*OF,* 114)

The primary architectonic metaphor of the first half of the novel is paintings of ugly, vicious people and of human cruelty, through descriptions of the pictures of the twentieth-century German-American artist George Grosz and the nineteenth-century Spanish painter Francisco Goya. Stevie then launches an attack on the murderous cruelty of the English, the Russians, and other peoples as a general indictment of humankind.

Suddenly, in midbook, the tone and style shift radically from a peripatetic, sardonic stream of consciousness to a first-person, action-filled account of love and war. Pompey, as if in a dream, is tricked into uniform and military service by her soldier-lover, Tom Satterthwaite, an English intelligence officer. Dressing in the dark, Pompey avoids looking at herself in the mirror, but finally, by fire light, she sees a reflection of an inner as well as an outer self: "The flames on the hearth shoot up and their savage wild light is reflected at my collar, is held reflected and thrown back with a light that is more savage, but completely savage, with the flick of a savage quick laughter the light is tossed back again from the stars upon my collar and the buckle at my waist. . . . I am in uniform" (*OF,* 217).

Published just before the outbreak of World War II, *Over the Frontier* shows what was happening psychologically to European women, as Stevie foreshadows and predicts their massive employment in uniform and the conditioning needed to get them to hate their fellow humans so that like Pompey they are able to shoot to kill. With the deadly partnership of men and women in war, a substitute for, as well as a metaphor of, women and men in bed, women are irrevocably changing: "Oh if there is to be anything of pleasure at all in the sweet use of heterosexuality, please remember to be feminine, darling Miss or Mrs., but once out of bed, pursue your own way" (*OF,* 152). Intelligent women will make their own independent way in the new world "for intelligence is sexless and has its own weapons . . . and if the women are clever in the way I have said to make the best of both worlds, the men . . . can afford to laugh. . . . It is a game" (*OF,* 151).

Stevie and Pompey predict that in postwar Britain, when military work is finished, a more androgynous kingdom will emerge: "Never again in England I think shall we breed exclusively masculine and exclusively feminine types at any high level of intelligence, but always there will be much of the one in the other" (*OF,* 149).

Pompey and Tom are lovers, couriers, secret agents, and competitors in the service of an archbishop and a generalissimo in an oneiric war against an unnamed totalitarian state. The author and her protagonist are opposed to any totalitarianism, but politics interest them far less than people. Back in Britain Pompey is asked by "Professor Dryasdust," "Are you not interested in politics, in working for peace, in the fight against fascism?" (*OF,* 256). Pompey's reply is, "No, I am not interested to concentrate upon politics, fascism or communism, or upon any groupisms whatever. . . . *C'est la vie entiere que c'est mon metier*" (*OF,* 256). All totalitarianisms are wrong. All ideologies are equally banal. As an artist, finally, Stevie's subject is people. Politics, economics, psychology, are only interesting in their use as means to understand human beings. Although Stevie does not explicitly relate their sexual acts, Pompey and Tom are energetic, often tender, sometimes angry lovers. On their mission across the frontier between the warring parties they "sleep by day and ride by night" (OF, 226). The constant riding, sometimes together, sometimes Pompey alone, symbolizes the erotic adventure of a formerly sexually conservative English girl. When the lovers are together, Pompey sometimes is wearing the uniform that converts her into someone hard, fierce, and aggressive; but sometimes she wears a feminine nightgown. Thus the frontier crossed over again and again is the sexual border between the traditional male and female roles and sexual positions. The amorphous border is ultimately the fading border between the psyche and the libido. At the same time, Pompey risks her life and is in mortal danger as she crosses a geopolitical border and thus she is like Hermes (Ca[s]milus) crossing back and forth from life to death, in and out of Hades, during her six-month adventure on the razor's edge.

Stevie is not as hard on women in Over the Frontier as she is in Novel on Yellow Paper. Her heroine, Pompey, here can cope, compete, and succeed in the male-created world of war. Still the English suburban housewife gets a raking:

Why do some women like to be bullied? . . . Now, at home where my aunt and I live, the wives are so often delighted to tell you how splendidly bullying their husbands are, and how they put the foot down here and there, and no, they will not let them play bridge in the afternoon and they will not let them smoke. 'My dear husband does not like to see me smoke', there is a great deal of pride in their voices when they say this. I have often noticed it, it is as if they would say, You may not think it but I am married to a tiger. No, I did not think it . . . for certainly no better disguise for a tiger exists anywhere than the disguise of a Bottle Green [Palmers Green] husband. (OF, 215)

In the latter and more fascinating half of Over the Frontier, which may be only a dream sequence, Pompey paradoxically devalues her gender by adopting the traditional masculine military role and simultaneously degenderizes that role. She can perform the warrior tasks only when in the ritualized costume, at which time she is transformed internally into an androgynous combatant. Pompey recognizes the epicene nature of her being as she encounters a mirror that reflects her psyche as well as her body (*OF*, 217). Thus she is able to shoot without regret the "rat face" enemy (*OF*, 249–50). In the end Tom belittles and leaves Pompey, jealous of her success in "his" world. He is unworthy of Pompey, who, like her creator, must face hostility in all areas not considered traditionally the province of women. But Pompey knows work must go on, and women must take and use power despite the unsettling effect on traditional men and women. The novels last words are: "Power and cruelty are the strength of our life, and in its weakness only is there the sweetness of love" (*OF*, 272).

In these respects *Over the Frontier* may be more vision than dream. Critics in the 1930s were perplexed by the midnovel shift from the interior mono-logue they had grown used to in *Novel on Yellow Paper* to the fantastic, surrealistic narrative of the second half. The reader today, aided by exposure to Stevie's poetry, almost all of which appeared in print subsequent to the publication of *Over the Frontier*, recognizes the controversial section as a near-poetic epic, a quest for gender indentification and role clarification by a female protagonist fleeing the dull, safe, stale, deadly boring world of peaceful suburbia across the border into tomorrow's inferno.

The Holiday

"Married to Death," a novel Stevie began immediately after finishing *Over the Frontier* and destroyed after her friend and editor David Garnett described it as unreadable, probably extended Pompey's story, because at the end of *Over the Frontier* she is awaiting further action. Garnett warned Stevie not to continue to write about herself,[4] but that is basically what Stevie could do, and so in her next and last novel she reincarnates herself again as Celia.

The setting of *The Holiday*, which was first written during World War II, was shifted to the postwar years as time slipped by until 1949, when Stevie was finally able to find a publisher for it. As a result, it was imperfectly edited so that certain absurdities slipped through, as when Celia and Casmilus, her cousin and would-be lover, are on holiday near a lake into which drops a British fighter plane flown by a German trying to escape a year or more after the war was over.[5] Despite the difficulty of finding a publisher, and the need to revise persistently, *The Holiday* was Stevie's own favorite of her novels.[6]

Britain's wartime suffering, save only for continuing casualties, extended long after the cessation of hostilities. Food remained scarce and rationed, many veterans were unemployed, the cities were in ruins, and the empire was breaking up. Everyone and everything was threadbare. Gloom rather than joy over victory transcended. In the hovel, cousin Caz, an intelligence officer

like Tom in *Over the Frontier,* sums it all up: "I do not know . . . that we can
bear not to be at war" (*H,* 8). In war at least there is action, exhilaration, and
the bracing flow of adrenalin. Celia also feels "It was better . . . in the war.
Now it is flat, and the heart has gone out of it" (*H,* 183).
Unfortunately, *The Holiday* is the least interesting and satisfying of
Stevie's three novels. For one thing, Stevie ran out of things to fictionalize
from her life, and she tried to recycle in Celia the experiences she used for
Pompey. Second, she shows even less interest in clear exposition than she did
in her earlier novels. Also her diatribes and lectures on Indian independence,
British politics, the Russian army of occupation in Germany, the medieval
philosopher Boethius, and the educational system, along with the inclusion
of a short story of hers added like filler in a Victorian serial novel, all seem
gratuitous. Finally, *The Holiday* has less wit and humor than *Novel on Yellow
Paper,* and it holds less fascination than *Over the Frontier.*
     The Holiday is a love story and a tale of near incest. Celia, the narrator and
Stevie surrogate, works at an unnamed ministry and lives with her old aunt in
a London suburb. She takes a holiday to visit her uncle Heber, a vicar. Accompanying Celia is her cousin Casmilus, whom she loves passionately and
who loves her. Their mutual sexual attraction is fierce. They cannot marry,
however, because of an old family rumor, apparently true, that they have the
same father. They touch, they lie together, they caress, they torture themselves. They go horseback riding together and they share their suffering: "Caz
sinks his face on to my open hand: Oh, why do we cry; oh, why do we cry so
much?" (*H,* 155). In the end there is only despair. Celia attempts to drown
herself but Caz saves her. The holiday has succeeded in taking Celia away
from her job but not from her emotional and sexual need for Caz. Only death
can do that, and it fails her.
     The name Celia derives from the Latin *caelum* ("sky" or "heaven"). Celia is
much more ethereal than Pompey. She is also strangely incomplete. Stevie
has given Celia's cousin-lover, Casmilus, Pompey's last name. Like the earlier
novels, *The Holiday* is autobiographical, but here Stevie has divided her surrogate into a female and a male. Celia and Casmilus are both separated and
joined forever by the sin of their father. The implications are that the "heroine," specifically and generically, is an androgyne.[7] Thus in this last novel
Stevie implies, like Plato, that the male and female principles, separate in the
phenomenal world, long for their original, ideal state of unification. As men
and women close the psychological, cultural, and even economic distances
between them, they approach the natural ideal.
     Stevie continues the architectonic use of iterative emptiness and death im-
ages and references from *Novel on Yellow Paper* and *Over the Frontier.* She also

continues to swipe at friends in slightly veiled references. George Orwell, with whom Stevie had a troubled relationship, is piquantly satirized as a narcissist by being divided into two characters, Basil Tate and Tom Fox, the former being in love with the latter. Basil, like Orwell, served in the Spanish Civil War (1936–1939). His feeling for Tom "is not entirely a homosexual thing (and not entirely not); it is innocent so far as it goes, but innocent?— but juvenile" (*H*, 68). Again, being Stevie's friend could be a trying affair.

The *Holiday* depicts the bitter, carping, middle-class intellectual life Stevie knew so well. It praises friendship between women and it encourages women's independence. It also endorses the camaraderie of workers of both sexes. In the end, however, as the critic Hermione Lee says, "it is, principally, a document of suffering, a painfully close account . . . of Celia/Stevie's battles with despair."[8] As Celia's friend, Lopez, says of her: "You are married to Death and Hades" (*H*, 66).

Ultimately the subject of all three novels, *Novel on Yellow Paper, Over the Frontier,* and *The Holiday,* is womanhood. The theme: midcentury Western women are anguished and immobilized by the conflict between their sense of gender and their pendulous role in society.

Chapter Three
Not a Good Girl: Short Stories and Other Prose

As a novelist, Stevie Smith's career spanned thirteen years; as a prose writer, thirty-four. Besides the novels, Stevie wrote short stories and essays of significant literary merit. A discussion of her minor works—book reviews, introductions, and a one-act radio play—is beyond the scope of the present volume.

Short Stories

Stevie's ten published short stories (others did not see print) first appeared in magazines, newspapers, and anthologies, and one was first broadcast over BBC radio. They have been reprinted, with some of her essays and uncollected poems, in the anthology *Me Again*. The stories are satiric, atrabilious, self-referential, facetious, and wickedly funny. In tone they are similar to much of her verse: prose songs of acerbic and morbid misanthropy. Stevie wrote about childhood, thinly disguised actual friendships, and her perception of the disappointments of a decaying gentility.

"Surrounded by Children" (1939), a seven-hundred-word piece, is an adult nightmare fantasy of infantilism, taking place on a pleasant summer day in London's Kensington Gardens and Hyde Park, where fat, pink-cheeked children are playing. An "ugly old girl" with "wisps of grey hair carelessly dyed that is rioting out from under her queer hat" (*MA*, 26) comes on the scene. She is a caricature of Stevie as witch. She talks to herself until she comes to an empty baby carriage for a rich child. The ugly old girl is seduced by the security the pram offers her, and she climbs in and tears off some of her clothes. The ugly old girl then stabs herself repeatedly with her hat pin until she is "transfixed in grotesque crucifixion upon the perambulator" thinking "what fate is this, what nightmare more *agaçant* so to lie and so die, in great pain, surrounded by children" (*MA*, 27).

The persona's horrible and pathetic struggle is an attempt to try to climb back into a condition of infancy and to assume Christ-like martyrdom in front of the mocking enemy, the real children, of whom she is envious. A child is waiting within the old girl's body for a liberation that adult life cannot allow. No story of Stevie's has as much economy, impact, and poignancy as this finely crafted, but pathetic, psychological revelation.

"The Herriots" (1939) is Stevie's perception of marriage, an unhappy state she has escaped. In this brief story a "Bottle Green" girl named Peg Lawless lives with her aged great aunt and her dead mother's sister in another "house of female habitation." Peg falls in love with and marries Coke Herriot, who fails as a salesman, so the young couple go to live with his parents while awaiting the birth of their first child. There is immediate conflict between wife and mother-in-law. "Mrs. Herriot unquestioningly put the wishes of the men first. Peg had been brought up to think that men were to fetch and to carry. She felt that she had married into an Indian or Turkish family" (*MA*, 75).

A son is born. Husband and wife fight over the mother-in-law. Things go from bad to worse. Coke gives up a steady job to work in an amusement park. He is soon unemployed, and Peg takes a job as a companion to an old woman who loves to visit the cemetery. There the old woman tries to reconcile Peg to her sad lot with the thought: "There is only one way in which you can get away . . . and that is to die and be buried" (*MA*, 79).

"The Herriots" is one of Stevie's most pessimistic stories. Suburban life is denigrated. Married life is presented as a trap for young girls. They are better off with their own gender in the tribe of women. An old woman knows.

"In the Beginning of the War" (1942) is a three-page story originally written as a long passage in *The Holiday* and then omitted.[1] In it Stevie expresses her wartime patriotic pride. The girl persona rejects the intellectual cant of scholars and politicians in favor of the pure feeling of the common people. She writes "a jingo poem about it, 'For every blow they inflict on Jewry, And other victims of their fury, They ask for death on bended knee, And we will give them death and we, Will give them death to three times three' " (*MA*, 29). Stevie's slight animus and snobbery toward Jews have abated in the light of the suffering of European Jewry and in the wake of her realization of the danger to Britain and democracy everywhere posed by the Nazis.

"A Very Pleasant Evening" (1946) is ironically titled, for the evening described is not at all pleasant. Rather, it is a gossipy, backbiting, drunken dinner party among middle-class intelligentsia, during a German air attack late in the war. After the party, the married host makes a pass at Lisa, the heroine, as he is escorting her to the underground station:

In the dark patch outside the lighted tube station Roland fell suddenly upon Lisa and began to kiss her. Oh Roland, how furious you are, sighed Lisa, as he gasped and panted. His right arm went round to the back of her shoulder, he caught hold of her hair and took a pull at it, forcing her head back, it was a furious adroit grip. Lisa began to laugh, Oh Roland, she said, and put her arms round him and kissed him, now I must go. . . . Good-bye Roland dear, Lisa drew apart and shook him politely by the hand. Thank you for a very pleasant evening. (MA, 34).

The surprising sensuality at the end, and Lisa's laughing, superior, amoral response to Roland's clumsy assault is the spice of the story. It is as if Stevie were saying: now they finally get down to basics.

"The Story of a Story" (1946) is a longer piece in which the protagonist, Helen, a writer who works for a publisher, pens a story about friends, a married couple, the husband of which violently objects to her writing about them and threatens to sue for libel. Helen can only think of her craft when Bella, the wife, says:

"he will have his solicitor write to you, . . . that if the story is published he will at once bring a libel action against you."
"It is so difficult to get these stories right," said Helen, her thoughts moving off from Roland to the dear story that was now at last so right, so truly beautiful. (MA, 53)

"The Story of a Story" is an allegory on the inability of friends of writers and even the general reading audience to realize that an artist must use her experience as grist for her creative mill. She has no choice. What others perceive as malice or abuse of friendship must be considered the license of art. The friends' view is always: "You go into houses under the cover of friendship and steal away the words that are spoken" (MA, 57). Helen, however, is upset by her friends' insensitivity and vindictiveness. In the end a pusillanimous editor withdraws the offer to publish and everything is lost: friendship and art.

"The Story of a Story" is drawn from real-life experiences of Stevie's. A story called "Life and Letters" was accepted for publication in May 1945 by the editor of *Modern Reading*, who, learning that it was about a friend of Stevie's, sat on it for over two years before apologetically returning it.[2] Another story, "Sunday at Home" (originally titled "Enemy Action"), had been accepted for publication in early 1946 for an anthology called *The Holiday Book*, but the editor, fearing a libel action after learning that it was based on an actual acquaintances of the author's, returned it. Stevie struggled to place the story and finally got it on the BBC, where it was broadcast on 20 April 1949.

"Sunday at Home," a six-page satire on middle-class marriage, concerns an eccentric couple during World War II. Ivor is a brilliant scientist who has been wounded in a bomb experiment. When German bombs begin to drop on London one day, they remind him of the experiment, so he climbs into a cupboard and talks to his nearly hysterical wife through the door. When the raid is over, he returns to his typewriter murmuring to himself, "How happy, how happy to be wrapped in science from the worst that fate and females could do" (*MA,* 45).

Gloria, his wife, is not highly educated. She is also depressed by the marriage: " 'Sin and suffering,' she cried now to herself. . . . 'Sin, pain, death, hell; despair and die. The brassy new world, the brassy hard-voiced young women. And underneath, the cold cold stone' " (*MA,* 46). She finds some solace with a female friend, but Ivor is always returning to run into the cupboard when the bombs drop.

"Sunday at Home" is as funny as any of Jules Feiffer's dark satires on family life. Marriage is shown to be for the husband an arena of freedom and for the wife a prison in which she toils as a domestic and must humor the whims and eccentricities of her mate.

"Is There a Life Beyond the Gravy?" (1947) is a wonderfully zany piece in which, as in *The Holiday,* the heroine is named Celia. Uncle Heber appears again, and there is another cousin Caz—not Casmilus, but Casivalaunus, the name of an ancient king of Britain. Celia works in a ministry office, where there is little to do, and she, Caz, and another cousin, Tiny, go on holiday to Heber's parish house where they revert, surrealistically, to childhood. Their lives are so desperately bland that they are barely alive. Celia says, "There's no room here for anyone who doesn't know he's dead" (*MA,* 73). All of them come to a grim realization: " 'We're all dead,' cried the three children. . . . 'We're all dead, we've been dead *for ages*' " (*MA,* 73).

"Beside the Seaside: A Holiday with Children" (1949) is another satire about middle-class family life and another lightly veiled attack on some of Stevie's friends. In this longer story the protagonist, Helen, a poet, is spending a beach holiday with her friends, a Jewish family. The story has a charming, lyrical beginning and ending. The locale is set: "The beach shelved steeply and the deep water lay in to shore; the water was also clear, you could see the toes of the paddlers, perched like fishing birds upon the upper shingle, knee deep in the water" (*MA,* 13).

Helen quickly finds herself at odds with a precocious ten-year-old, Hughie, who is loud, bossy, and already a male chauvinist. Despite protestations to the contrary, Helen does not care much for Hughie's father, who is detached from his family and frets as to whether or not he should take off his shirt at the seashore. He finally does, but quickly dons his hat again. Helen's true friend is the wife, Margaret, who, although also Jewish, complains that her tense husband is "more locked up in being a Jew than it seems possible" (MA, 19).

Margaret fears that there may be concentration camps some day in England. Helen blames the Jews: " 'One sometimes thinks that is what they want,' said Helen flippantly, getting rather cross, 'they behave so extremely' " (MA, 19). Stevie is here reflecting the anger shared by many Britons over the attacks on British troops by Jews then fighting for the independence of Israel from the mandate power and from the Arabs. She is unsympathetic with Zionism, she has forgotten the Holocaust, and as a political conservative she is cross with the nationalistic aspirations of such people as the Indians, the Irish, and the Kenyans, among others, all of whom had struggled or were struggling to free themselves from colonialism and establish independent states.

Helen; Margaret; Margaret's likable daughter, Anna; and another female friend finally escape from the men by going on an outing. They have a wonderful time among themselves, but when they return they are faced by a furious Hughie: " 'You are low, disgusting women,' he said in a low, fast voice getting louder, 'You are liars. I curse the day I was born' " (MA, 23). He becomes hysterical, and Margaret finally must subdue him by swatting him across the shin with a rolled up copy of Life magazine. Delighted to see the male rival struck, Stevie/Helen wickedly sums up the holiday thus: "Oh, what a pleasant holiday this was, how much she had enjoyed today for instance; hitting Hughie had also been quite agreeable" (MA, 25).

The world is clearly better for women when men are kept in their place: a separate and distant one. Stevie also implies that male children must not be permitted to cultivate their sexual imperialism from an early age.

In "To School in Germany" (1955) the protagonist, again a woman, remembers when, before World War II, she was a sixteen-year-old schoolgirl in Potsdam and courted by a Jew-baiting, English-hating young man named Maxi, whom she turned down precisely because he was German. The second part of the story takes place many years after the war. The woman sees Maxi in the British zone of allied-occupied Germany and identifies him to a cousin in the army who realizes that Maxi is a hunted war criminal. He turns him in, and because his record was "vile beyond words," Maxi gets a fifteen year sentence. The protagonist says: " 'How beastly and bitter it all is: I hate this "holier than thou" situation we are all in now.' 'We ARE holier than him,' said my cousin" (*MA*, 38).

Stevie never forgave the Germans for their embracing of fascism and their attack on western civilization. In contrast, after the British withdrew from Palestine and after the establishment of the state of Israel, Stevie grew less baffled by and frustrated with Jewish anxiety in a hostile world.

In the brief "Getting Rid of Sadie" (1955) Stevie investigates the hearts of children and finds them little different from those of adults. Here a brother and sister learn that their former governess has been convicted of "attempting to extort money by menaces" (*MA*, 39). They recall how a few years earlier they had planned to tie her up and threaten to drown her if she did not turn over her savings to them. They never attempted their extortion by menace because the dress rehearsal using the family dog failed when Prince became ill from terror. At the end the children wonder if they "would really have pushed her in" (*MA*, 43).

Stevie implies that these "angel infants" have enough original sin in them to commit any evil. Young children are amoral. Only with the strictest of education is their any chance of humanizing and civilizing them. Even then it may not be possible.

After 1955 Stevie no longer wrote short stories. The genre had never been of primary importance to her, and she always had trouble placing them for publication. Stevie's stories are more snapshots than narrations. They offer small but acute insights into individual characters, and they illuminate quite specific situations. Usually, however, they say even more about Stevie, almost always the true narrator-protagonist, than they do about the revealed characters. Thus Stevie's stories in a sense competed with her poems. They cover the same ground, but her skills as a poet were far greater. The ultimate value in studying Stevie's stories resides in discerning the way they bridge her novels and her verse, essentially by exploring poetic themes and ideas in prose, almost as prose poems. Simultaneously, they have biographical value as indicators of Stevie's feelings toward friends, children, marriage, and middle-class British life in general.

Essays

Stevie's varied essays deal with poetic inspiration, biographical and circumjacent aspects of her life, writing techniques, religion, and the accessibility of death. Her essay style is lucid, personal, and friendly; she is less cynical and biting than in her fiction and verse. One is left with the distinct impression that if Stevie Smith had written an autobiography it would have been very different indeed from any portrayal of her personality by friends, observers, or scholars.

"Private Views" (1938) is an essay on the annual summer art show at the Royal Academy in London. Stevie is less concerned with the pictures than she is with the building and, especially, the patrons: "In physique the people who throng the galleries are all rather tall, except for some of the ladies who are rather thin, but still tall, so that for all this it is a little difficult to come near to the pictures or the wall" (MA, 131).

"Mosaic" (1939), as the title implies, is a short essay covering much ground. First it depicts life with her aunt and her neighbors in what Stevie calls "Bottle Green." Stevie and the Lion Aunt do not have a radio because Mrs. Spears does not like "the noise," and so they listen to the news at a neighbor's house. Most of Stevie's suburban neighbors do not realize the gravity of the German threat in 1939. They try to excuse and justify the Nazi abuse of old Jews in Vienna who when forced to scrub pavements "did not laugh; you see they did not take it in the right spirit" (MA, 106).

In this essay the perspicacious and sensitive Stevie is aware that war is imminent, that the soft, happy-go-lucky, "peace pledging" sons of the suburbs will soon be fighting and dying, and that a great evil is emanating from Germany. Most important of all, Stevie argues that men and women "are not good and evil in essence, but in the sum of their actions they are good and evil" (MA, 107). Thus all of us are personally responsible for our own actions, and none can excuse individual crimes in the name of the state.

"Syler's Green: A Return Journey" (1947) is a charming reminiscence of Palmers Green when Stevie as a child was brought there from Hull by her mother and aunt. It was more of a country place than a suburb: "a very beautiful place to live in, especially for young children. There were fields to play in and shady country lanes, and farm houses with their cows and the pigs" (MA, 84). Stevie relives her schooldays in prose and poetry, and she shows her undying love for the community in which she grew up and lived out her days.

"A London Suburb" (1949) is a description and sociological survey of a typical London suburb much like Stevie's own Palmers Green. The essay updates "Syler's Green," viewing suburban life more critically than earlier essays did. After describing the rail connection, the architecture, and the religious and social organizations, Stevie turns to the inhabitants whose snobbery she lambastes: " 'Mother,' says the child, 'is that a dog of good family?' She is pointing to a puppy bull-dog of seven weeks old" (MA, 103).

Like Émile Zola, Stevie dissects the houses and finds unhappy marriages, dirty children, and violent parents. Still:

The virtue of the suburb lies in this: it is wide open to the sky, it is linked to the city, it is linked to the country, the air blows fresh, it is a cheap place for families to live in and have children and gardens: it smells of lime trees, tar, cut grass, roses, it has clear colours that are not smudged by London soot. . . . In the streets and gardens are the pretty trees—laburnum, monkey puzzle, mountain ash, the roses, the rhododendron, the lilac. and behind the fishnet curtains in the windows of the houses is the family life—father's chair, uproar, dogs, babies and radio. (*MA,* 104).

"Too Tired for Words" (1956) is an intelligent and sensitive person's cry to omnipotent physicians that death as well as life must be respected for some people would "storm back through the gates of Birth" (*MA,* 117). Stevie also points out here that even the errors produced by weariness have creative potential as when she accidentally wrote *lobster* for *lodestar* and began a poem "Duty was my lobster, my lobster was she," which made it all the more interesting to her (*MA,* 111–12). Here again Stevie mixes poetry and prose and takes the opportunity to get some excellent verse, including "Not Waving but Drowning," into print at a time when she was having difficulty finding outlets for her poetry.

"History or Poetic Drama?" (1958) is Stevie's contribution to a book celebrating T. S. Eliot's seventieth birthday. Surprisingly, since both she and Eliot work out of the Anglo-Catholic tradition, Stevie attacks the great literary arbiter on historical and theological grounds even as she expresses admiration for his poetic gifts and his powerful imagery. She argues that Eliot's *Murder in the Cathedral* does not depict its hero, Thomas Becket, with historical veracity. Eliot has romanticized Becket and villainized the secular forces of King Henry II to create "rather something ignoble, a flight from largeness into smallness, a flight in fear to a religion of fear, from freedom to captivity, from human dignity to degradation" (*MA,* 149). Stevie despised the meekness and mortification of medieval Christianity as she hated the doctrine of eternal damnation used to invocate fear, "for fear is degrading, and we are counselled, for our soul's good, to fear. Is this the truth of philosophy and religion?" (*MA,* 149).

"History or Poetic Drama?" is Stevie's most brilliantly intellectual essay. It is a key to her view of Christianity as a stoic communion with a difficult God in a hostile universe. Stevie categorically rejects a fearful, unquestioning subservience to a theology, just as she rejected subservience to a political tyranny.

In "My Muse" (1960), a two-page prose poem, Stevie describes her muse:

"She is an Angel, very strong. . . . She makes a strong communication. Poetry is like a strong explosion in the sky. She makes a mushroom shape of terror and drops to the ground with a strong infection" (*MA*, 126).

"Simple Living" (1964) is a short essay the purpose of which is "to show the enjoyment that lurks in simplicity" (*MA*, 108). Stevie extols the virtue of regular habits, looking at colors, looking at animals, and having a glass of sherry daily.

"At School" (1966) is an essay enfolding a seventeen-stanza narrative love poem also titled "At School," in which a pair of school-age lovers ride horses and kiss as they ride, reminiscent of Pompey and Tom in *Over the Frontier*. They also cry a great deal and ask: "Oh why do we cry so much?" (*MA*, 123) a line straight out of *The Holiday*. In the prose part of the essay Stevie discusses her education in classic literature. She argues that memorization of great poetry is good for children. She then shows how she would teach her own poem, "At School," to a class. Although Stevie speaks warmly of children both in the poem and in the pedagogical discussion, she rather gives the game away as she discusses the homework her imaginary class would turn in: "Well, I would read them some time—chiefly to see if these ideas of mine had come through to any of the children, and then, and only of very secondary interest I fear, to see what ideas, if any, the little beasts might have of their own" (*MA*, 124).

The first version of "Some Impediments to Christian Commitment" was written in 1957 and published in the Oxford University undergraduate journal *Gemini*. A later, fuller version, presented as a lecture to the Saint Anne's Society in 1968, is Stevie's most direct and comprehensive statement of her position on Christianity. It is an impassioned and paradoxically spiritual apologia for her sometimes agnosticism.

Stevie argues that although there can be no proof of a loving God's existence, there is no harm in behaving as if He or She did. Stevie is against assertions of certainty, however, because such assertions provoke anger with those who honestly do not agree. Furthermore, one can live in a world of doubt and still find love, joy, and satisfaction. To illustrate her ambivalence and her confusion over Christianity Stevie describes her childhood religious feeling and her deep and passionate love for church music and ritual. However, the cruelties of Christianity, the emphasis on the horror of the Crucifixion, the history of the Inquisition, and the interminable massacres, soon alienated her from "the beauties of Christianity" she identified with "as a child of Europe," for "Christianity was the religion of Europe" (*MA*, 156).

Finally, Stevie addresses the divinity of Christ. She examines Christ's message and meaning in both poetry and prose as she attempts to reconcile His words of love with the doctrine of eternal damnation. She concludes that perhaps "Christ was a poet and used Hell as a figure of the appallingness of becoming entirely sinful" (*MA*, 167).

"What Poems are Made Of" (1969) is Stevie's last discussion of poetics. She speaks of the preferred pain of isolation. Better isolation than commitments that erode creative concentration.

Poems come to Stevie through colors that "drive me most strongly, colours in painted pictures, but most strongly of all, colours out of doors in the fresh cool air" (*MA*, 127). Also she is moved to write poetry by the theological and historical books she reviews. Lastly, death inspires her. She asks, "Why are so many of my poems about death, if I am having such an enjoyable time all the time?" (*MA*, 128). Her ultimate answer: "I love Death because he breaks the human pattern and frees us from pleasures too prolonged as well as from the pains of this world. It is pleasant, too, to remember that Death lies in our hands; he must come if we call him" (*MA*, 129).

Some Are More Human Than Others

Although she never took herself very seriously as an artist, Stevie loved to draw. Generally her drawings were supplementary or complimentary to her poems, but sometimes she drew for the pleasure of the process and did not juxtapose the drawing with a poem. Instead, it received a caption, like a cartoon.

In 1958 Stevie found a London publisher, Gaberbocchus, willing to bring out a collection of seventy-six of her drawings, most of which are accompanied by wryly humorous and sometimes profound captions. They are in English, French, or German. Many are mere doodles, and some are cruelly self-deprecatory. *Some Are More Human Than Others* (1958) is close in effect to the cartoonlike satire of James Thurber, who, like Stevie, combines the line and the word as integrated co-signs of artistic communications. The collection shows, as much as any of Stevie's essays, how the woman saw herself and how much more she cared for domestic animals than she did for domesticated humans.

Cats in Colour

Cats in Colour (1959) is a delightful picture book for cat lovers with humorous captions and an introductory essay that warns readers against the vain condescension of anthropomorphism. Cats have minds, but we do not know them, so we make up stories about them and superimpose our own feelings on them. Then we "turn in disgust, if they catch, as they do some-times, something of our own fevers and unquietness" (*CC*, 7).

Stevie shows her love and respect for animals: "I think all animal life, tame or wild, the cat life, the dog life and the tiger life alike, are hidden from us and protected by darkness, they are too dark for us to read. We may read our pets' bellies and their passions, we may feed them and give them warmth; or, if we are villains, we may kick them out, ill treat them. . . . But still they are not ours, to possess and know, they belong to another world and from that world and its strange obediences no human being can steal them away. It is a thought that cheers one up" (*CC*, 8).

Stevie's essays evidence the depth and breadth of her excellent basic edu-cation and her extensive reading in classic literature, philosophy, theology, and history. Along with her poems and fiction, but much more directly, they form a moving autobiography. More significantly, they offer an aesthetic in which the true poet is defined as one who is fiercely honest, who is concerned with heaven and hell, life and death, and good and evil, and who is ulti-mately aware that her self is secondary to her art.

Chapter Four
Beware the Man: Early Poetry

Seamus Heaney notes that Stevie Smith's concerns were central ones: "Death, waste, loneliness, the maimed, the stupid, the innocent, the trusting."[1] As a poet she expressed these concerns in an original manner. "Gradually she came to be recognized as a very special poet of strangeness, loneliness and quirky humour."[2] Stevie Smith is an acquired taste. Levity, loneliness, poignancy, mockery, aspirity, and raw polemics make for a heady draught. Ultimately, the serious reader cannot admire enough "the wide range of her subject matter, . . . her profound human insight, . . . her religious quest, her lyrical magic, . . . her gift for comprehension, . . . her astonishing technical mastery."[3]

As a technician Stevie has a strong sense of the line and is extremely competent in the various forms of English poetry from the ballad and the hymn through free verse. A nineteenth-century trait is Stevie's use of narrative poetry, the dramatic monologue, and character sketches. She writes in iambic pentameter, eight-stress trochaic tetrameter, and even hendecasyllables. Very frequently she employs a long conversational line with the rhythms of a particular class's speech woven into it to blend colloquial language with poetic feeling. As in neoclassic English verse she likes to create suspense and surprise with her couplet endings. Rhymes, full and half, internal and end, are the primary means she employs for controlling the line and creating humor. Alliteration, assonance, and startling, concentrated, seemingly juxtapositional monosyllables support her shocking constructs. She is a genius of densified diction. The flow and spontaneity of her verse is often enchanting.

A Good Time Was Had by All

In the seventy-six-poem collection *A Good Time Was Had by All* (1937) Stevie initially presents the three voices she was to develop and refine in her career as a poet: the elfin child and adolescent girl, a representation of innocence departing; the lonely, cynical woman, a representation of malison; and the stoic philosopher, a representation of wisdom. *A Good Time Was Had by All* also introduces the main subjects of her poetic canon: childhood, adolescence, the relationship between the sexes, parent and child, animal life, God and religion, and death.

The title *A Good Time Was Had by All* is an ironic one. The "good time" referred to is that of Eros, but no character in a poem, and especially not the protagonist, is having much of a good time. It is all very ambivalent, as in the ballad "Barlow":

> I'm growing much fonder of Barlow
> And I think of him a lot
> And sometimes I think I'm in love with him
> And wish that I was not.[4]

Or it is depressing, as in "Forgive me forgive me": "Forgive me forgive me for here where I stand / There is no friend beside me no lover at hand / No footstep but mine in my desert of sand" (*GT,* 19).

In "Progression" the persona has fallen in love with Major Spruce, "The sweetest major in the force," but soon, alas, "he's grown such a bore," so Stevie kills him off and presents an unfeeling epitaph: "He was the last of the Spruces, / And about time too" (*GT,* 20). She accompanies the poem with a humorous drawing of the major expiring on his death bed.

"The Hound of Ulster," which opens *A Good Time Was Had by All,* is a key poem in the volume. Innocence, represented by a young boy, is confronted with an opportunity for experience and is fearful. A voice says:

> Little boy
> Will you stop
> And take a look
> In the puppy shop—

The wise and suspicious child hesitates and asks; "But tell me I pray / What lurks in the gray / Cold shadows at the back of the shop?" Fate rewards the child's suspicion with survival:

> Little boy do not stop
> Come away
> From the puppy shop
> For the Hound of Ulster lies tethered there
> Cuchulain tethered by his golden hair.
> (*GT,* 9)

The animal waiting at the end of the experience is no pet but the tragic hero and epic sufferer of Irish myth. The lesson from adult experience, the voice of the poem, taught to the child, is that one never knows what destiny has in store and thus the best way is the cautious, untrusting way. Similarly, in "Heber" a child adapts an old nursery rhyme to deal with her own pet or her own fantasy monster:

> I love little Heber
> His coat is so warm
> And if I don't speak to him
> He'll do me no harm.
>
> (*GT*, 15)

In "From the Greek" the persona has adult knowledge but a child's voice: "But the worst fate of all (tra la) / 's to have no fate at all (tra la)" (*GT*, 28).

"Little Boy Lost" reminds the reader of William Blake's "The Little Boy Lost" and "A Little Boy Lost" in that all these poems evoke the child's fear of loss or separation from parents, but Stevie's elfin boy has a kind of maturity and stoic acceptance of his situation:

> Did I love father, mother, home?
> Not very much; but now they're gone
> I think of them with kindly toleration
> Bred inevitably of separation.
> Really if I could find some food
> I should be happy enough in this wood.
>
> (*GT*, 65)

The child's voice blends under the pressure of necessity into the voice of the stoic, for in this world at any moment an innocent child may become a refugee waiting, as in "Louise," "on an upturned valise," thinking, "Oh if I could stay / Just for two weeks in one place" (*GT*, 96). Childhood in Stevie's early poetry is only a brief train stop on the route between innocence and experience, credulousness and cynicism, birth and death.

Calvin Bedient says, "Death stood in for Stevie's father; she looked up at it, ran to it when she was hurt, needed its love."[5] *A Good Time Was Had by All* introduces Stevie's lifelong obsession with death, an obsession that, naturally enough, darkens from volume to volume. Yet always death provides sustenance; it is the emergency ration in the soldier's pack: just being there, it helps get you through. Death also is the welcome relief that permits a retreat over the border from an unpalatable world into oblivion.[6]

In "The River Deben" the poet contemplates the sweetness of drowning, although in the end death "comest unwanted" (*GT,* 51). In "Up and Down" the busy world depresses Stevie, and she is impatient for her death: "I shall be glad when there's an end / of all the noise that doth offend / My soul. Still Night, don cloak, descend" (*GT,* 27). She contemplates suicide in "Does No Love Last?":

> I see in fancy
> My body spread
> That in a frenzy
> Down I cast.
> 'Tis broken now and bloody.
> Does no love last?
> (*GT,* 66)

When the world disappoints, death is always an option. In "Never Again"

> When I have had enough
> I will arise
> And go unto my Father
> And I will say to Him:
> Father, I have had enough.
> (*GT,* 64)

In "Death Came to Me" Stevie explores several ways to commit suicide. The act can also be considered a selfish one. Excessive concern for oneself through prolonged psychoanalysis can lead to depression and ignoble suicide as in "Analysand" where the subject "chases his tale like a puppy-fool" until:

> All thoughts that are turned inward to their source
> Bring one to self-hatred and remorse
> The punishment is suicide of course
> (*GT,* 57).

Infrequently, Stevie laments death, as in "Night-Time in the Cemetery": "Yet stand I by my grave as they by theirs. Oh bitter Death that brought their love and mine unto a coffin's breadth" (*GT,* 25).

Basically, Stevie's view of death in *A Good Time Was Had by All* is simple and unencumbered theologically. The spirit confiding to "Mrs. Simpkins" states: "Death's not a separation or alteration or parting / it's just a one-handled door" (*GT,* 17). "The Reason," however, does introduce Stevie's life-long antinomal critique of God: "It is because I can't make up my mind / If God is good, impotent or unkind" (*GT,* 55).

Stevie is ambivalent in her feelings about the necessary but difficult relationship between women and men. In the autobiographical "Papa Love Baby," the title is both baby talk by the child persona and an importunity, but the poem disparages both parents:

> My mother was a romantic girl
> So she had to marry a man with his hair in curl
> Who subsequently became my unrespected papa
>
> . . . .
> I sat upright in my baby carriage
> And wished mama hadn't made such a foolish marriage.
>
> . . . .
> . . . later papa ran away to sea.
>
> . . . .
> I could not grieve
> But I think I was somewhat to blame.
>
> (*GT,* 11)

However, another poem, "Alfred the Great," accompanied by a sketch of an expressionless man with a large moustache, standing before a waving clothes line, praises the man who accepts responsibility for a family: "Honour and magnify this man of men / Who keeps a wife and seven children on £2 10" (*GT,* 14).

Still, in "Eng." Stevie asks in the voice of the cynical, lonely woman:

> What has happened to the young men of Eng.?
> Why are they so lovey-dovey so sad and so domesticated
> So sad and so philoprogenitive
> So sad and without sensuality?
>
> (*GT,* 46)

In other words, why are they all married and so damn domesticated and unsexy? The despicable, bisexual "Major Macroo," who has several boy friends, abuses "his patient Griselda of a wife" (*GT,* 46), and she accepts it with masochistic uncomplaint. Brute men also murder innocent girls, as in "Bag-Snatching in Dublin," where "A bruiser in a fix / Murdered her for 6/6" (*GT,* 49). As for marriage in general, the autobiographical

"Freddie" snaps: "People who say we ought to get married ought to get smacked" (*GT,* 69).

In her poetry as in her novels Stevie expressed dissatisfaction with the lack of substance and sexuality in "This Englishwoman": "This Englishwoman is so refined / She has no bosom and no behind" (*GT,* 73). Stevie is also hard on the soldiers who survived World War I in "Bandol (Var)":

> In the south of France, my dear
> Is full of the most awfully queer
> Majors of the British Army, retired.
> . . . .
> And they say
> Quite in the best stage-army traditional way:
> "England was quite a good place to live in before the War Hawkahaw."
> They all seem to have got catarrh.
>
> (*GT,* 12)

In a Good Time Was Had by All Stevie presents her enduring fondness and respect for animals. God chastises humankind in "Nature and Free Animals": "I will forgive you everything, / But what you have done to my Dogs / I will not forgive" (*GT,* 43). Stevie sings to the dog "Belvoir," and she laments the "Death of the Dog Belvoir," who was "of beasts best" (*GT,* 67).

In the beginning of her lifelong literary struggle with Christianity, Stevie, in "Sunt Leones," praises the lions over the Christian martyrs. It is the lions who create the martyrs and thus the Church: "And if the Christians felt a little blue— / Well people being eaten often do." Thus "our debt to Lionhood must never be forgotten" (*GT,* 59).

The most charming (if I dare use that term) page in *A Good Time Was Had by All* is that which includes the illustration for the couplet "All things pass / Love and mankind are grass" (*GT,* 58).

The poems of *A Good Time Was Had by All* are protean and sardonic. Stevie had spent ten years in writing them. They are bold, clear, witty, unexpected, and often brilliant as light. She triumphantly creates an image and persona of mock innocence. The collection is as auspicious an inaugural work as Robert Frost's *A Boy's Will.*

Tender Only to One

With sharp wit and surprising sentimentality, Stevie jokes, laments, parodies, and sings her way, like Lear's Fool, through her second collection. She

All Things Pass

All things pass
Love and mankind is grass.

fights a guerrilla war with the threatening male voice, the straw man of the absent father, and the slave-lover-god: death. Of the sixty-six poems in *Tender Only to One* (1938), twenty-seven are death poems.

The title poem, "Tender Only to One," is a lyric seemingly sung by the persona about a lover whose name she does not now know. In the little girl's guessing game of plucking petals from a daisy the loved one's name shockingly is revealed:

> Tender only to one,
> Last petal's latest breath
> Cries out aloud
> Fron the icy shroud
> His name, his name is Death.[7]

If the collection *Tender Only to One* is primarily about any subject, it is about death.

In "Come Death," the first of two poems by that title in the Stevie Smith canon, the poet berates death in King Jamesian English for his delay: "Why dost thou dally, Death, and tarry on the way?" (*TO*, 22). She reproves Christ for installing fear of death:

> How foolish are the words of the old monks,
> In Life remember Death.
> . . . .
> How vain the work of Christianity
> To teach humanity
> Courage in its mortality.
> Who would not rather die
> And quiet lie
> Beneath the sod
> With or without a god?
>
> (*TO*, 22)

Life is a foolish illusion more to be feared than death. Religious beliefs keep us from peace.

Although Stevie's interest in death has the ring of late Victorianism, it is never lachrymose or lugubrious. In her most serious mind, Stevie's sense of life is tragic. Like King Lear on the heath, she desires the extinguishing of life itself, evidenced in "Will Ever": "Would that the seas lay heavy upon the dead, / The lightless dead in the grave of a world new drowned" (*TO*, 70).

Like a seventeenth-century metaphysical poet, Stevie, in "Proud Death with Swelling Port," atypically rages against death for first taking the brightest and the best:

> Proud Death with swelling port comes ruffling by
> He takes the worthy and leaves the fond
> So many worthy men and they must die.
> And all the foolish men stay still behind
> The shadow of Death's beckoning.

Cynically, Stevie exhorts death to be more selective for the good of humankind: "Oh spare them Lord, take toll of lesser men, / For it is certain *they* will never come again" (*TO*, 42). In "Proud Death with Swelling Port," Death, a friendly servant in other poems, becomes a spoiler.

In the illustration for "The Toll of the Roads," three angels weep over and pray for an accident victim whose brains are splattering the road while a motorist drives unconcernedly away. Stevie often draws angels and iteratively refers to them in her verse. Arthur C. Rankin says, "The frequent appearance of the Angels indicates a preoccupation with sin, censure and punishment."[8] Ironically, in "The Toll of the Road" the angels are asking of the victim: "Oh what is come upon him to make the road his death-bed?" (*TO*, 11), as if he chose to die in the street. Angels just can't figure us out.

"In Canaan's Happy Land" finds Stevie playing sardonically on the patriotic hymn "Jerusalem," based on the preface to William Blake's *Milton*, which ends with "Till we have built Jerusalem / In England's green & pleasant land." In the poem a veteran of World War I is now a cursed peddler, but he recalls:

> The bells ring for my friends
> Who were untimely slain,
> But I was luckier than they
> And go my rounds again.
> (*TO*, 41)

Survival is good, too, and, having come through the maelstrom of modern warfare, the veteran is unperturbable.

A wise but gravely ill boy in "Nourish Me on an Egg" understands the full cycle of life:

Nourish me on an egg, Nanny,
Don't wring your hands and weep,
Bring me a glass of stout
And close my eyes in sleep.
(*TO*, 50)

Death can by faced with equanimity even by a child. Another ill child, in "Little Sick Boy," becomes Blake's "Tyger" as his illness destroys his body:

I am not God's little lamb
I am God's sick tiger.
And I prowl about at night
and what most I love I bite.
(*TO*, 15)

Once more Stevie calls upon the seas to drown all, but "they will not do it," for persons must abide "Death's Ostracism" (*TO*, 16). The lyric "The Boat" finds a girl learning that her dead lover desires her to join him in death by suicide. She decides: "Come death within my hands and I / Unto my love will go" (*TO*, 17).

The old green "Parrot" in his dingy cage, like a worn out old man, is "sick with malevolent rage" as he suffers and waits for the mercy of death:

. . . His feathered chest
knows no minute of rest.
High on his perch he sits
And coughs and spits,
Waiting for death to come.
Pray heaven it wont be long.
(*TO*, 18)

"The Doctor" asks a patient: "Do you find that the pain is more than you can bear?" The patient asks for a drug and then plans to:

. . . hide
Somewhere on the seashore where the tide
Coming upon me when I am asleep shall cover
Me, go over entirely,
Carry beyond recovery.
(*TO*, 19)

The song "Upon a Grave" finds a mother thinking of her son in the grave where "worms his flesh divide" (*TO*, 58). And in "Bye Baby Bother" a mother asks Bother where is his brother? He is dead and Baby Bother plans revenge in a general mobilization for war. The mother realizes that "Dozens by hundreds will be taken and torn," and she ruefully cries "Oh would the day had died first when you were born" (*TO*, 59).

The final comment on death is a light one as Stevie contemplates a "Suicide's Epitaph" and jocularly addresses God and her reader:

> Oh Lord have mercy on my soul
> As I had none upon my body.
> And you who stand and read this rhyme
> How do you do, Tomnoddy?
>
> (*TO*, 72)

Death, no matter how lightly treated, is a somber subject. The realm of male-female relationships and the role of women in the male-dominated British society of her time provide Stevie greater opportunities for wit and her own kind of fun. Stevie's work on these themes makes for the most entertaining and contemporary experiences in *Tender Only to One*. A young man in "I Hate This Girl" dislikes a girl who "is so cold." In fact, he "should like to kill her" but, as will happen, libido takes over: "But what do I do? / Kiss her, kiss her, / And wish that she would kiss me too" (*TO*, 20).

"Infelice" is the devastating tale of a masochistic woman in love with "Sir Rat," who treats her like a doormat. The more he mistreats her, the more she deludes herself that his abuse is a sign of his love. Rejection is always denied, even when

> He lies down beside me, his face is like the sand,
> He is in a sleep of love, my heart is singing.
> Sleeping softly softly, in the morning I must wake him,
> And waking he murmurs, I only came to sleep.
>
> (*TO*, 21)

Implied in "Infelice" is not only male manipulation and cruelty, but also male sexual inadequacy.

"The Murder" is accompanied by a drawing of a dead woman in the arms of a man. An indifferent parrot looks on. The man has just "closed her eyes in death." Like the duke in Robert Browning's "My last Duchess," he has killed his love because "She was not like other girls—rather diffident, / And that is how we had an accident" (*TO*, 31).

In "Mother, among the Dustbins" Stevie remembers her dead parent, asking her "what lies behind: death?" She answers the question herself: "Naught but the vanity of a protesting mind / That would not die." But the "presence of God," more important than the pronouncements of humans, can be felt "in the broom / I hold, in the cobwebs in the room, / But most of all in the shadows of the tomb" (*TO*, 32). It is death that assures us of God's existence.

"Le Désert de L'Amour" and "Arabella," two poems about the death of love, are turned into satires by the clever illustrations. "Dear Karl" is autobiographical, like "Freddie" in *A Good Time Was Had by All*. The poet sends her lover a sixpenny selected edition of Walt Whitman's poetry and is defensive because she knows he will be indignant over having to accept the impostion of an editor's choice. It is, however, her only Whitman and all she can afford. She urges Karl to enjoy it "between lunchtime and dinner. Bon voyage, Karl, bon voyage" (*TO*, 40). Thus the poem criticizes his rigidity and egotism as it says farewell with a gift. Implied is a permanent break in an unsatisfactory relationship.

The funniest poem in *Tender Only to One* is "Dear Female Heart," a clerihew addressed to the suffering that accompanies love:

> Dear Female Heart, I am sorry for you,
> You must suffer, that is all you can do.
> But if you like, in common with the rest of the human race,
> You may also look most absurd with a miserable face.
>
> (*TO*, 45)

The poem is accompanied by a humorous sketch of a slim, dishevelled girl in a slip trying to do up her stringy, recalcitrant hair and looking frustrated. Poem and picture together argue for a simple acceptance of humanity.

In the six-stanza lyric "La Gretchen de Nos Jours," the first of two poems in the canon with the same title, the poet, in her young girl's voice, regrets the loss of her lover. "In foolish wrath" she has "Driven him ever / From my path." Alas:

> Never shall love
> Untimely slain
> Rise from the grave
> And live again.
>
> (*TO*, 49)

Stevie's adolescent girl persona—of whom the critic Hugh G. Porteus says, "Her typical Miss . . . is aged about fourteen"[9]—reappears in the penultimate poem of *Tender Only to One*. There she is torn between two "lovers": "One is my father / And one my Divine." She asks the key question: "Which shall I follow . . . / And following die?" Her answer to both "loves" and to the world is: "No longer count on me / But to say goodbye" (*TO*, 76). Stevie's animal friends are not forgotten in *Tender Only to One*. "O Happy Dogs of England" advises: "Bark well at errand boys / If you lived anywhere else / You would not be allowed to make such an infernal noise" (*TO*, 8). The poem is an allegorical satire by conservative Stevie on the unappreciativeness of her fellow British in regard to their political freedom.

Anthropomorphized, the rodent in "To a Dead Vole" is:

> . . . done in all thy bleeding.
> The soul is sped
> And all thy body's heeding
> For daily bread
> And comfortable bed
> Has brought thee where there's no thought of feeding,
> And where the soil is thy last unappreciated quilt.
>
> (*TO*, 36)

The human animal can expect no more nor less.

Two poems in the collection deal with Stevie's craft. "Souvenir de Monsieur Poop" is a monologue by a prejudiced literary arbiter or critic. He is "an old fogey," quite

> . . . prepared to go to the stake
> For Shakespeare, Milton,
> And coming to our own times,
> Of course
> Housman
>
> (*TO*, 53).

By considering this Victorian-Edwardian poet modern, he reveals his oblivion to truly modern movements in art and of course, to young, new poets such as Stevie Smith.

"Dear Muse" is a direct epistolary address in which the poet expresses love for her creative source, wishing only that "sometimes you would speak louder, / But perhaps you will do so when you are prouder" (*TO*, 51).

Tender Only to One is darker, more philosophical, than *A Good Time Was*

Had by All. The elfin child's voice had been somewhat muted, and the voice of the cynical, lonely woman emerges more clearly and strongly. With the publication of a second book of verse in one year's time it became quite clear that Stevie Smith was not "in danger of sinking back, like a character in one of her poems, beneath the waves of oblivion,"[10] even though the only one she was tender to was death.

Mother, What Is Man?

The title of Stevie's third collection derives from Francis Thompson's long poem, "An Anthem of Earth" (1894):

> . . . Ay, Mother! Mother!
> What is this Man, thy darling kissed and cuffed,
> Thou lustily engender'st,
> To sweat, and make his brag, and rot,
> Crowned with all honour and all shamefulness?[11]

Stevie's choice of these lines by an important late-Victorian religious poet indicates her ambivalence toward men and even toward the mothers who make them.

Mother, What Is Man? (1942) marks the full growth of the elfin girl-child voice into that of the lonely, cynical woman. The first of the seventy-five poems in the collection, "Human Affection," is one of the last poems in the voice of the child persona. In "Mother" the child is transmogrified into an adult who uses a child's voice to mock her mother:

> I have a happy nature
> But Mother is always sad,
> I enjoy every moment of my life,—
> Mother has been had.[12]

The mature voice looks back in "Girls!" and admonishes young women sardonically, "although I am a woman / I always try to appear human" (*M*, 15). To be human is to suffer. But as Patricia Meyer Spacks states in *The Female Imagination,* girls soon "learn to know that their suffering derives from gender rather than from common humanity."[13] Stevie would have agreed with that statement.

In the second "La Gretchen de Nos Jours" the persona suffers as she waits passively, hoping for her lover to return, but knowing:

> Hope and desire,
> All unfulfilled,
> Have more than rope
> And hangmen killed.
>
> (*M*, 13)

The lonely, cynical persona continues to seek companionship and love regardless of the cost. "In the Night" finds her bitter: "And now in the desolate night / I think only of the people I should like to bite" (*M*, 57). And friends may be worse than death, as in "Dirge": "I do not fear the night above, / As I fear the friends below" (*M*, 36). In "The Broken Heart" the need for love leads to tragic results:

> The roses are withered,
> But here on my breast, far
> Redder than they is
> The red of my heart's blood.
>
> (*M*, 55)

The unattractive persona in the clerihew "The Sad Heart" believes pitifully and falsely: "I never learned to attract, you see, / And so I might as well not be" (*M*, 33). She has never learned that self-worth need not depend on physical makeup, that female misery over a supposed lack of beauty is a cruel manifestation of the debilitating standards men have imposed on women.

In great pain the lonely persona cries out to the inanimate as well as the animate world for love, but her cry goes unheeded. She shouts "Love Me!":

> Love me, Love me, I cried to the rocks and the trees,
> And Love me, they cried again, but it was only to tease.
> Once I cried Love me to the people, but they fled like a dream,
> And when I cried Love me to my friend, she began to scream.
>
> (*M*, 41)

Accompanying the poem is a sketch of four sad, naked women rejecting a fifth.

"The Actress," ostensibly about a thespian, is really about the cynical woman's persona. Although here she earns her bread upon the stage, amid painted scenery, she, who "weeps and toils" in the "world of wood," insists, "I have a poet's mind, but a poor exterior, / What goes on inside me is superior" (*M*, 49). It is important to note that the cynical woman's persona keeps a tight rein on her expressions of loneliness, and she usually, but not always, is able to maintain her self-esteem. "Lot's Wife" suffers not only because it is

her fate but also because of her knowledge. She suffers stoically, knowing that
"Though a marriage be fairly sprung, / And the heart be loving and
giving, / In the end it is sure to go wrong." Her answer is to pursue her destiny and find dignity as well as comfort in oblivion:

> Then take me to the valley of asphalt,
> And turn me to a river of stone,
> That no tree may shift to my sighing,
> Or breezes cover my moan.
>
> (M, 64)

One must "Study to Deserve Death," but as in "Conviction (iv)" a woman
must also study living and enjoy the arms of men, being "held and tightly
kissed," and she must learn to:

> . . . like to laugh and be happy
> With a beautiful beautiful kiss,
> I tell you, in all the world
> There is no bliss like this.
>
> (M, 27)

The voice of the philosopher rises in *Mother, What Is Man?* Stevie can seem to espouse religious orthodoxy, as in "Conviction (i)," where she has "For God a hymn of praise" (*M*, 26). In "Conviction (ii)" she is unafraid of the Hound of Hell: "I knew my Lord was risen again,— / Wild dog, wild dog, you bark in vain" (*M*, 26). She can sigh for "The Heavenly City," and in "The Repentence of Lady T," when the face of vanity is seen by the persona, she begs, "Oh Lamb of God / Change me, change me" (*M*, 51). Stevie's skepticism and misanthropy, however, are always waiting in the wings. In "More People," illustrated by an angel with a glum look on her face, the persona is a bomber pilot, "son of mischief's lover," who flies to "drop my bomb upon a church steeple" (*M*, 67).

Stevie has great sympathy for the beasts. If they are predators, then her sentiments are for them and not their victims. In "The Zoo" the old, caged lion weeps "tears of ruby rage": "He does not like you little boy / It's no use making up to him" (*M*, 20). But the lion's day is over and he is trapped:

> His claws are blunt, his teeth fall out,
> No victim's flesh consoles his snout,
> And that is why his eyes are red
> Considering his talents are misused.
>
> (*M*, 21)

Nature has designed the noble lion as a killing machine. It is cruel to cage him and prevent his instinctive behavior: "God gave him lovely teeth and claws / So that he might eat little boys" (*M*, 20).

"The Wild Dog" is uncaged. Unlike the "City Dog" he does not need socialism to "keep his tail stiff." His life is free: "He goes to the river, he stamps on the mud, / And at night he sleeps in the dark wood." The clever city dog, on the other hand, drinks at the trough, is on the "brink of human intelligence," and knows that if worse comes to worse "the Council will give him a drink" (*M*, 42).

Mother, What Is Man? asks a question which Stevie sardonically answers in "A Man I Am":

> I was consumed by so much hate
> I did not feel that I could wait,
>
> . . . .
>
> I ran into the forest wild,
> I seized a little new born child.

I tore his throat, I licked my fang,
Just like a wolf. A wolf I am.
(*M*, 54)

To indicate that she is talking about men and not mankind, Stevie illustrates
the poem with the head of an ugly man.

The collection's last poem, untitled in *Mother, What Is Man?* but later, in
Collected Poems (1975), called "Torquemada," offers an oblique answer to the
title question. The piece is really a captioned cartoon showing the wry-faced
Grand Inquisitor walking with a little girl and a dog. The child asks, "Uncle
Torquemada, / does Beppo know about Jesus?" (*M*, 81). She and the dog
are innocent; so is the question. But the implication is that the beast may
know more about charity than the man.

It may be, however, despite the collection's cynicism, skepticism, misanthropy, and obsession with death, that the poem "If I lie down," illustrated by
a child in a sleep suit, but with an adult's face, standing next to her bed in a
room with a Crucifix on the wall, sums up all the attitudinal voices of Stevie's
early books of poetry—the child's, the woman's, the philosopher's: "If I lie
down upon my bed I must be here, / But if I lie down in my grave I may be
elsewhere" (*M*, 24).

Stevie Smith's first three books of poetry, produced at the same time she
was writing and publishing two novels and working on a third, are a part of
one'of the great explosions of energy in twentieth-century British letters. It is
as if a vast burst of flak hit the sky and, descending, washed the literary air of
much posing, pedantry, obscurism, and mendacity. As Philip Larkin says of
these earlier works, Stevie "sees something more where we do not, takes a pot
shot at it, and when she holds it up forces us to admit that there was something there, even though we have never seen anything like it before."[14]

Chapter Five
Touch and Go:
Poems of the 1950s

In her poetry collections *Harold's Leap* (1950) and *Not Waving but Drowning* (1957) Stevie strove for an even greater simplicity of diction, an outward shift of feeling, and further development of character poems in which she projects her weltanschauung and her growing desire to escape from her grinding, nine-to-five, middle-class suburban life, and even from existence itself. The cynical, lonely woman persona grows older, sharper in voice, and more despairing in outlook. A title from *Harold's Leap* comes close to summarizing the overriding feeling of much, but not all, of these two volumes: "Deeply Morbid." The collections solidify that unique quality in Stevie's verse which Joyce Carol Oates calls the "eerie spell."[1]

Harold's Leap

Escape is the major theme of *Harold's Leap*: escape from circumstance and escape to death. The title piece of the sixty-five-poem collection praises the successful attempt at suicide by one who "was always afraid to climb high," admiring the courage it takes: "It was a brave thing to do." Stevie philosophically asks: "Would you?"[2] Of course she is as curious about her own reaction to that key question as she is to ours.

The poem "I Rode with my Darling . . ." reads like a synopsis of the second part of *Over the Frontier.* Two lovers ride "in the dark wood at night." The male wishes to leave the dangerous place. He is being "responsible," but the female is determined "to stay with the angel in the dark wood at night." The angel is death and the wood is oblivion. The woman rides on alone to the end, escaping love, lover, and family:

> Loved I once my darling? I love him not now.
> Had I a mother beloved? She lies far away.
> A sister, a loving heart?

> My aunt a noble lady?
> All all is silent in the dark wood at night.
>
> (*HL*, 42)

Anemone in "Voices about the Princess Anemone" is another girl who "ran into the forest wild / And there she lay and never smiled" (*HL*, 81). The persona accepts and clarifies the dominant role of fear in life for "Fear is a band of gold." Fear possesses the princess persona and yet is also a source of inspiration for her—and for Stevie.

In "Friskers, or Gods and Men" a girl is turning Kafkaesquely into a cat, but she is not unhappy, for a cat's life may be better than her own: "I shall be most loved of all the young cats" (*HL*, 51). The accompanying drawing shows a young woman transmuting into a feline.

"Do Take Muriel Out" starts lightly. A female friend, the persona, is trying to get her a date with a gent:

> Do take Muriel out
> She is looking so glum
> Do take Muriel out
> All her friends have gone.
>
> (*HL*, 32)

Five stanzas later the reader is shocked to learn that the man importuned is death:

> Do take Muriel out
> Although your name is Death
> She will not complain
> When you dance her over the blasted health.
>
> (*HL*, 32)

Another kind of escape, besides death, for the lonely woman persona in *Harold's Leap*, is escape into a fantasy of the prehistoric world at the time of the dinosaurs. If only time

> . . . but stopped then
> Oh had there not come men.
> In that high and early time
> There was no good deed and no crime
> No oppression by informed mind
> No knowledge and no human kind.
>
> (*HL*, 70)

People run away, or threaten to run away from their circumstances in "Cool as a Cucumber" and "Lightly Bound." In the former, "Mary" went to a wishing well, but a fairy "came up out of the well / And cursed her up hill and down dale / And cursed her from midnight to morning hale" (*HL*, 22). The curse, ironically, is the gift of an independent mind. "She is never grim and bold." This naturally makes her "quite unfit for marriage." When a lover does come for her she runs away. "She has not been seen since then. / If you ask me she'll not be seen again" (*HL*, 22). Marriage thus is something to be fled.

In "Lightly Bound" a fed up wife tears into her husband and child and threatens to run away:

> You beastly child, I wish you had miscarried,
> You beastly husband, I wish I had never married,
>
> . . . .
> Do you suppose I shall stay when I can go so easily?
> (*HL*, 49)

"A Wretched Woman" has not escaped her marriage and is shown crying over her frying pan while an ugly girl child pounds on her back. She is miserable because of her "lack of household craft" (*HL*, 48). Contrarily, the girl in "The Hat" thinks a beautiful hat will bring her a king to marry, for marriage is the only meaning for her life. In "The After-thought" Rapunzel's lover is calling to her to "let down your hair." He is coming with a rope ladder so that when he climbs her hair to her chamber they both will be able to "escape into the dark woods immediately" (*HL*, 38). Again, the lover who takes the persona into the woods is death.

"Mr. Over" "is dead." Sardonically, Stevie uses wartime communications lingo in a search for God: "He died fighting and true / And on his tombstone they wrote / Over to You" (*HL*, 44). Stevie wants to know "who is this beautiful You?" However, at the poem's end "a devil's voice cried: Happy / Happy the dead" (*HL*, 44). Gnostic dualism is implied. God and the devil, good and evil reside simultaneously in us all.

For the poem "My Cats" Stevie drew a picture of herself dressed as a witch flying on a broomstick with a cat riding pillion. That image and the many poems about death, murder, and suicide provoked an anonymous *Times Literary Supplement* reviewer to call Stevie a witch, not one being burned herself, "but having her characters find their own murderous or suicidal stakes."[3] Stevie was not unhappy with the appellation. In the last poem of *Harold's Leap*, "The Ghost of Ware," Stevie presents herself as a ghost and illustrates

the piece with an ethereally smiling woman's face. She cultivates the super-
natural connection not literally, of course, but within the ancient and quite respectable concept of the artist as inspired creator.

She certainly invents a crazed world in *Harold's Leap*, the kind a malevolent psychopath with a sense of humor might come up with: a girl is happy to
be turned into a cat; in "The Leader" the "squirrel brings nuts and the mole
brings meal" to him (*HL*, 75); a Christian asks a lion to eat her in "The
Roman Road" (*HL*, 9); a famous and worthy man is murdered by an angel in
"The Crown of Bays," who follows the knife with a verbal cut too: "In my
opinion for what it is worth, you die trivially" (*HL*, 62); and "A Jew is Angry
with his Friend who does not Believe in Circumcision" and tries to circumcise
and castrate him (*HL*, 66).

Confusion reigns in this slightly mad world of *Harold's Leap*. A child
seems to be saying "our dog is dead" in "Our Bog is Dead," but Bog turns
into God: "They bowed their heads. Our Bog is ours / And we are wholly
his" (*HL*, 47). Language obfuscates instead of clarifying: "For what was
dood, and what their Bog / They never could agree" (*HL*, 47). Humans
cannot agree on the nature or even the existence of God. Pantheistically, God
may be nature itself, and the spirit of God, as in the earlier poem
"Torquemada," may reside in the animals Stevie loves.

Other ghosts besides "The Ghost of Ware" march through *Harold's Leap*.
In "The Wanderer" the persona speaks of a "pityful" ghost, illustrated by a
long-legged, lean, wild-haired girl. The ghost is "pityful" because she does
not realize that death is better than life, and "She is happier far where the
night winds fall, / And there are no doors and no windows at all" (*HL*, 39).
The uncle ghost in "Le Revenant" knows "It is much better to be dead." He
tries to tell the living, but "they stoned him from the door" (*HL*, 50).

"The Weak Monk," a shifty and suspicious-looking fellow in his illustration, is on his way to bury a book he has written because "It was not according
to Catholic doctrine." The book's title is "Of God and Men."

> . . . he thought he'd a right to expect that God
> Would rescue his book alive from the sod.
>
> Of course it rotted in the snow and rain;
> No one will ever know what he wrote of God and man.
>   (*HL*, 33)

So much for literary immortality, especially if you won't take your chances
and publish.

Ten pages after "The Weak Monk" Stevie's poem "God and Man" appears. Now Stevie has God beg humans not to commit suicide even though they despair: "Oh Man, Man, of all my animals dearest, / Do not come till I call, though thou weariest first" (HL, 43). It is as if Stevie has been advocating suicide too strongly and is pulling back a little. Stevie remains ambivalent about suicide as about so much else.

Perhaps the saddest poem in *Harold's Leap* is the semiautobiographical "Deeply Morbid," the story of Joan the lonely typist with a "look within her eye" that always seems "to say goodbye." At lunch time, "solitary," she goes to the National Gallery to "watch the pictures." Finally one day, as she is gazing at a painting by Joseph Turner, the hold that her colleagues and friends have on her weakens and the picture captures her. She translocates to

> . . . the painted shore
> And there she walks for ever more
> Happy quite
> Beaming bright
> In a happy happy light
> All alone.

> They say she was a morbid girl, no doubt of it
> And what befell her clearly grew out of it
> But I say She's a lucky one
> To walk for ever in that sun
> And as I bless sweet Turner's name
> I wish that I could do the same.
>
> (HL, 84)

Escape here is adumbrated: the world of art, madness, or death. Suddenly and unexpectedly at the end of the poem the reader learns that what appeared to be a straight narrative by the poet is in fact a dramatic monologue by a persona envious of Joan's fate.

Somewhat self-pitying is "The Orphan Reformed" in which an orphan girl "roams the world over" looking "for parents and shelter," crying "Father, Mother" at various couples. Finally she realizes that she has been rebellious and that to be alone is her fate: "Now when she cries, Father, Mother, it is only to please. / Now the people do not mind, now they say she is a mild tease" (HL, 23).

Of course not all of the poems in *Harold's Leap* are direful. Conservative Stevie spoofs the Irish literary renaissance and Irish nationalism in "The

Celtic Fringe" by implying that both practitioners and supporters are a little cracked:

> Kathleen ni Houlihan
> Walking down the boule-igan
> Ran into a hooligan
> Ah ha, Kathleen ni Houlihan.
> (HL, 74)

Stevie's satirical poems etching the comic elements of the human condition have instant impact. "A Mother's Hearse" is about a spoiled boy who has "his will at every turn." He becomes so grasping, so selfish that

> His eyes do burn with a hungry fire
> His fingers clutch at the air and do not tire
> He is a persecuting force
> And as he grows older he grows worse.
>
> And for his sake the friends are put down
> And the happy people do not come round.
> (HL, 16)

Finally, the persona concludes that a mother's love "were better a mother's hearse." For emphasis Stevie includes a sketch of a smug-looking boy peering down on a horse-drawn hearse. Stevie was probably writing about personal experience with friends and their families here and also in "The Broken Friendship," where a friendship between two women breaks up over tea because one sits mutely when the other cries, "My heart is dull of despair" (HL, 36).

In "Pad, pad" a man, shown with a fallen face, remembers the moment a girl, shown with prominent breasts and with flowers in her hair, rejects him. He has suffered, but now: "Ah me, the power to feel exaggerated, angry and sad / The years have taken from me, softly I go now, pad pad" (HL, 35).

Again there is an autobiographical feeling in the poem, as if Stevie were describing the plight of a former swain. The poet feels guilty toward the persona and thus assuages his pain in the poem, if not in life. She is telling him and the world that time brings perspective and healing to all who give their hearts in vain.

In "Full well I know" the persona castigates another writer who has a "flinty heart / That beats beneath those gentle airs." That woman invites people to her home not out of love but only to observe them. Stevie implies that she herself would never do that. Her final judgment here is that art must emerge from the process of caring for people: "Then also as a writer she must fail / Since art without compassion don't avail?" (*HL*, 80).

"To School!" finds the poet persona attacking the "Prize Asses," that is, those critics who award prizes and would have "all the little poets be gathered together in classes." Stevie implies that she does not want to be classified or placed in a school of poetry, for one cannot "expect the Muse to attend this school" (*HL*, 53). Thus "To School!" is a plea by Stevie to be left out of the perennial lumping, sorting, judging, and categorizing of poets.

"From the Coptic" is presented as a creation myth purportedly from the Hamitic language of the early Egyptian Christians, the Copts. In it, three angels, as in a Medieval morality play, address

> . . . red and white clay
> Where in heaps it formless lay
>
> Stand up, stand up thou lazy red clay
> Stand up and be Man this happy day.
> (*HL*, 67)

But Man does not want to stand up and be a man. Rather, he seems to be asking: "Who needs it?" Two angels work on Man but to no avail, until the third talks him into it: "I am Death, said the angel, and death is the end, / I am Man, cries clay rising, and you are my friend" (*HL*, 68). Only death makes life worth living, but the reader wonders, why bother in the first place?

Similarly, in "The Deserter," when a friend says that the persona is "a deserter to ill health," implying that she willfully perpetuates illness, she calls the friend "Portentous ass" and decides: "I shall quite simply never speak to the fellow again" (*HL*, 41). The persona loves her "illness," real or imaginary. When one is ill and doctors and nurses keep you "in bed under observation," it is a comfort and an escape. Attention is what it is all about.

Harold's Leap has two long story-poems, both of which focus on death by gunshot. In "A Shooting Incident" Colonel Yeast of the British Indian Army is in the jungle hunting tiger, but also remembering remorsefully his dead dog Bunce, whom in his dreams or perhaps in life he has beaten to death. Yeast finds it easier to cope with wild animals. He shoots the tiger "through the teeth," but the memory of the loving pet is unbearable:

> And so my dog would look at me
> And it was pitiful to see
> Such love an such dependency.
> The human heart is not at ease
> With animals that look like these.
>
> (*HL*, 26)

The Englishman and men in general cannot handle being loved. Yeast realizes: "We slay the thing we most do love," a line similar to Oscar Wilde's "each man kills the thing he loves." Finally out of guilt or out of a belated realization of the unity of life and the equal value of all animals, the colonel shoots himself to death.

"Who Shot Eugene" is another restatement of the iterative riding episode in *Over the Frontier.* This time the persona is the man. He and Eugenie, both secret agents, have ridden for three days. Finally, in "the grey of an early day" they dismount, water their horses, have breakfast, and lie down to sleep "The sleep of exhaustion." Then:

> The sun was hot on my face when I woke, and Eugenie was dead,
> Shot, with a bullet through her head.
> Yet every chamber in her revolver was full to plenty
> And only in my own is there one that is empty.
>
> (*HL*, 79)

The poem's end is a shocker. Who else but the man could have shot Eugenie, and why did he do it? The clue is earlier in the description of his dreams, which are about "hostile Nature" and "Of forests deploying and advancing with the power of death." The persona blends his metaphors of war with his concept of nature and he perceives nature as his enemy. Eugenie, a woman and a comrade to love, must be murdered because the persona, like Colonel Yeast, cannot bear to be loved. The harsh primal meaning of both these shooting poems lies in the answer to the question, what do men do? Generically and genetically they kill. Yeast and Eugenie's lover are men. Naturally, they have been created to kill, not to love.

"No Categories!" and "Do Not!" are the two most philosophical poems in *Harold's Leap.* In the former Stevie prays "To God who created me / Not to you angels who frustrated me" (*HL*, 40). Angels have "severe faces" and "scholarly grimaces," and they are full of "appropriate admonishment." Angels are plodders, and they block direct communication with God. Stevie wants "No hierarchies I pray." She pleads for a simpler religion without the interference of would-be intermediaries like priests.

"Do Not!" is Stevie's poem of advice. It is illustrated by a drawing of teeming people. She preaches that people are basically alike, and an individual, regardless of "Sadness for failed ambition," should "not despair of Man, and do not scold him." She calls upon us, and by implication herself, to "know your own heart, that heart's not wholly evil." As they are basically alike, so humans are basically good. We all desire to be loved and are moved by beauty to virtue. "If judge you must, but with compassion see life" (*HL*, 71).

Harold's Leap is a look into the dark heart of humanity, but it presents a perspective that is not without understanding and compassion. Although Stevie excoriates her compatriots and her class, she cares for them deeply. Although she is grateful for the existence of death, she does not pander to the comforting concept of a humane, forgiving, merciful, immortality-providing God any more than she accepts the doctrine of eternal damnation. Still, Stevie talks to God as if the deity were there, and her message is "I doubt you very much." With *Harold's Leap* it becomes clear that, as Michael Tatham states, Stevie Smith is "one of the few religious poets of our time."[4]

Not Waving but Drowning

In the sixty-eight-poem collection *Not Waving but Drowning* (1957) Stevie takes even greater risks than she did in *Harold's Leap,* treading the sometimes thin line between whimsy and profundity as she plies her now perfected trade in what Muriel Spark describes as "curious chit-chat rhymes, elongated lines, comic metrical arrangements and mordant phrases."[5]

In this, her finest collection, Stevie exceeds all her previous efforts to electrify simple, flat words—those worn, barely audible, barely noticeable signs of the English language—into full relief as conveyors of concentrated feelings such as emotional pain, tenderness, sadness, loss, and despair.

The triadic persona flourishes in *Not Waving but Drowning,* but the philosophical voice is stronger than before. New themes emerge: concern for the writer's duty to fulfill the promise of her talents, and disdain for critics and writers who cling to old and obsolete values.

The title poem is Stevie's most famous. In it a drowned man protests to a living acquaintance, "I was much further out than you thought / And not waving but drowning."[6] He is pleading for understanding, but his friend thinks he was fooling around and went too far: "Poor chap, he always loved larking / And now he's dead. It must have been too cold for him." The dead man moans in frustration:

Oh, no, no, no, it was too cold always

. . . .

I was much too far out all my life
And not waving but drowning.

(*NW,* 13)

The dead and the living cannot communicate, but the living do not do much better with one another. No one wants her actions misunderstood or her life misinterpreted, but it is inevitable. Furthermore, it is dangerous to be different and it is deadly to take risks. We are dying all our lives. Living itself is a kind of suicide. The humorous dimension of "Not Waving but Drowning" is macabre. The deceased persona's indignation at being misunderstood is grotesquely as well as pathetically amusing.[7]

Significantly, the last poem in *Not Waving but Drowning,* "Farewell," also presents a dying persona. She has loved friends, but most of her affection is for the natural world:

Farewell dear world
With the waters around you curled
And the grass on your breast
I loved you best.

Farewell fish and insect
Bird, animal, swift mover
Grim reptile as well
I was your approver.

(*NW,* 76)

Death, unmentioned specifically, is merely a departure, a "Farewell / As a sweet bell."

Stevie's child persona appears only occasionally in *Not Waving but Drowning* and almost entirely in the four cat poems. The delightful pair "Nipping Pussy's Feet in Fun (This is not Kind)" and "Cat Asks Mouse Out (But Then Neither is This)" are accompanied by a drawing of a little girl seemingly reaching out to pinch a cat. The latter poem is spoken by a cat, exhorting "Mrs Mouse" to "come out of your house" and "bring the little mice too" (*NW,* 52). People are cruel to cats and cats are cruel to mice. So goes the world.

"My Cat Major," on the following page, is a hunter too. A young woman is sketched with a worried face, watching the supercilious feline. He has his deep, dark, animal secrets:

> Oh Major is a fine cat
> He walks cleverly
> And what is he at, my fine cat?
> No one can see.
>
> (*NW*, 53)

In "The Singing Cat" a pet cat carried in a box by his mistress on a train is released from captivity for a breather and wonderously begins to sing. The ballad sounds biblical or King Jamesian as onlookers show their astonishment at the miracle:

> He lifteth up his innocent paw
> Upon her breast he clingeth
> And everybody cries, Behold
> The cat, the cat that singeth.
>
> He lifteth up his innocent voice
> He lifteth up, he singeth
> And all the people warm themselves
> In the love his beauty bringeth.
>
> (*NW*, 62)

Two other animals, both dogs, inhabit *Not Waving but Drowning*. One is a performing dog. Stevie hates the idea of animals being trained to entertain humans. In "This is Disgraceful and Abominable" she says, "Animals are animals and have their nature / And that's enough, it is enough, leave it alone" (*NW*, 39). She has seen "in a French circus":

> A performing dog [who]
> Raised his back leg when he did not need to
> He did not wish to relieve himself, he was made to raise his leg.
> Weep for the disgrace, forbid the abomination.
>
> (*NW*, 39)

Surely Stevie must have been vehemently opposed to animal vivisection and experimentation.

"Jumbo," a house pet, is called in sickening terms by his mistress: "Jumbo, Jumbo, Jumbo darling, Jumbo come to Mother. / But Jumbo wouldn't he was a dog who simply wouldn't bother" (*NW*, 70). Although Jumbo is "an ugly beast with drooping guts and filthy skin," he nevertheless has his animal integrity. It is the human who begs and crawls.

One other poem in *Not Waving but Drowning* features the voice of the child or the child's perspective, but as an adult's dream or recollection. In "A Dream of Nourishment" the persona's infant face is pressed against her mother's breast. Suckling, the infant feels "the sun of strength beat into my veins." She is "all bursting, all delight." But in the end, "The breast was withdrawn violently / And oh the famishment for me" (*NW*, 44). The shock in this psychologically insightful poem is the traumatic withdrawal of the breast, cruelly or indifferently done, and the resulting lifelong sense of rejection in the cut-off persona. The grief is almost visible and the suffering nearly tangible.

The voice of the lonely, cynical woman resounds in *Not Waving but Drowning*. The persona in "Look!" passionately cries out for attention, demanding to be looked at, to actually be seen:

> I am becalmed in a deep sea
> And give signals, but they are not answered
> And yet I see ships in the distance
> And give signals, but they do not answer.
>
> (*NW*, 64)

She does not know why she is shunned. That is the essence of her loneliness: is it her fault that she is a "leper" or "pariah"? She finds an interesting fish in the water but, alas, "who shall I show him to?" This ambivalence is expressed again and again in the full canon. She disdains marriage or commitment with any of the available supply of effeminate, sexually inadequate men, but simultaneously and antithetically she suffers from painful loneliness.

Most pathetic and moving is "Every Lovely Limb's a Desolation," in which the persona sees nature and the joys of life as if through the window of a moving train:

> I see the pretty fields and streams, I hear
> Beasts calling and birds singing, oh not clear
> But as a prisoner
> Who in a train doth pass
> And through the glass
> Peer;
> Ah me, so far away is joy, so near.
>
> (*NW*, 42)

However, the overriding feeling is of lonely despair: "All, all is isolation / And every lovely limb's a desolation" (*NW*, 43). The effect of the poem is not dissimilar to Samuel Taylor Coleridge's "Dejection: An Ode." Sadly, sometimes only stroking an animal's fur can provide solace and allow the persona to say "It Filled my Heart with Love."

In "Die Lorelie" the persona recalls the ancient myth of a beautiful, smiling woman who lures sailors to their doom. The persona wonders: "Lurks there some meaning underneath?" (*NW*, 75). The tale brings her much grief. But for what? For whom? The poor sailors or herself because she has no such power over men?

In her version of "Dido's Farewell to Aeneas" Stevie restates her perennial solution to rejection by life:

> . . . the dagger in her hand,
> I die unavenged, she cried, but I die as I choose,
> Come Death, you know you must come when you're called
> Although you're a god. And this way, and this way, I call you.
>
> (*NW* 33)

If all else is lost to the disappointed persona, there remains her control of life through the throttle of death.

In the clerihew "Longing for Death because of Feebleness," illustrated by a large angel leading a sleepy-looking Stevie angel in seeming first flight, the persona is exhausted from living with the weight of the flesh. The poem is an early indication of a rising concern in Stevie's writing: a fear of debilitation and dependency in old age. How much better if she could "leave the flesh to become a reliable spirit / Possibly travelling far and acquiring merit" (*NW*, 63).

"Longing for Death because of Feebleness" shares a page with "My Heart Goes Out," a prayer "to my Creator in love / Who gave me Death, as end and remedy" (*NW*, 63). Stevie insists that "All living creatures come to quiet Death," which is what they want "although / When they are living they do not think so."

The fine poem "The Hostage" is about a hostage Englishwoman who is to "hang at dawn." The time and place of the poem are unclear. Although she is Anglican, she allows a Catholic priest to relieve her heart by listening to her. In her "confession" she admits that "Even as a child . . . I recall in my pram / Wishing it were over and done with" (*NW*, 30). Her life has not been happy. She "never dared form any close acquaintance. / Marriage? Out of the question" (*NW*, 31). Her death wish and her despair perplex the priest, who cannot understand her pleasure in death, and whose final judgment reflects his confusion: "Well I see, said the Father, the case is complicated, / I will pray for you, Daughter, as I pray for all created / Meanwhile, since you want to die and have to, you may go on feeling elated" (*NW*, 31). Established religion is not equipped to deal with such an anomaly except as the priest says "Remember life not to cling to it." That is the moral position of the persona and her own state of grace.

The persona in "Away, Melancholy" strives to let it pass because all nature is one, and life continues both despite death and because of it, but she is not convincing in her argument. As long as humans are so difficult to comprehend, melancholy is incurable.

Two macabre poems that entwine martyrdom, the Crucifixion, and suicide are "God the Eater" and "God the Drinker." Stevie restates her agnosticism in the former: "There is a god in whom I do not believe / Yet to this god my love stretches" (*NW*,, 40). This god is not one who is consumed like Jesus, but one who provides oblivion through consuming:

> When I am dead I hope that he will eat
> Everything I have been and have not been
> And crunch and feed upon it and grow fat
> Eating my life all up as it is his.
>   (*NW*, 40)

"God the Drinker" is more active, but is the same devouring deity:

> I like to see him drink the gash
> I made with my own knife
> And draw the blood out of my wrist
> And drink my life.
>   (*NW*, 40)

Finally, in these apocalyptic poems, Stevie reveals the name of her god: "His name is Death."

In *Not Waving but Drowning* Stevie not only continues to voice opposition to the ill treatment of animals, but also speaks out against the destruction of natural terrain even when it is done in the name of progress and for human advantage. In "The Engine Drain" the altering of the fens through draining makes the persona unhappy despite the fact the engine creates "A fertile flat and farming land / A profitable farming land" (*NW*, 25). But the innocent waters of the mere are delivered mercilessly to the wash, to "the cruel salt sea"

(*NW*, 26). The fresh water of the mere is embittered by the salt of the sea, representing a loss of natural purity and even innocence. It is yet another betrayal to which the woman persona sadly relates.

The satiric pieces in *Not Waving but Drowning* are cutting, pointed, powerful, and often extremely funny. "Childe Rolandine," reminiscent of Robert Browning's "Childe Roland" and the unfinished ballad of Edgar in *King Lear*, "Child Rowland to the dark tower came," is illustrated by a drawing of a typist wearing a huge hat and sitting at her machine. The poem's "secretary-typist" sings "against oppression and the rule of the wrong." Her evil tower is the modern corporation headquarters, and "Dark was the day for Child Rolandine the artist / When she went to work as a secretary-typist" (*NW*, 35). How can the female artist survive as a creator in a world run by plutocrats, devoid of respect for the questing woman writer, and requiring her to do "work that is tedious for her daily bread"?

In "The Queen and the Young Princess" the princess persona is advised by her mother the queen to "embrace the headache and the crown / Marred pleasure's best, shadow makes the sun strong" (*NW*, 21). She must do her job and bear the necessary pain as her mother has done. To create or even see beauty in this world requires enduring the headaches that come with intelligence, ability, and responsibility.

The young woman persona in "My Hat" has been deluded by her mother into believing that wearing a certain hat would make her "certain to get off with the right sort of chap." Instead, it lifts her, like Peter Pan, into the sky and carries her to a desert island where "it's nice to be rid of Father, Mother and the young man" (*NW*, 23). Better to escape all the rigmarole and routine of courtship. The magic hat keeps her in "Never Never Land." It symbolizes poetic inspiration and it provides a living escape for the woman persona.

The beautiful "Fafnir and the Knights" is Stevie's profound "Puff, the Magic Dragon." Fafnir is a "Happy simple creature . . . / With a mild bright eye / And a waving tail." But the "Knights of the Advancing Band" come to kill the innocent and harmless dragon. His body is destined to be broken and torn "for a knight's merit." Tragically, nothing can be done to save the innocent and the natural in a world dominated by powerful men. The only succor is resignation:

> Fafnir, I shall say then,
> Thou art better dead
> For the knights have burnt thy grass
> And thou couldst not have fed.
> (*NW*, 29)

Typically, Stevie is on the side of the beasts. Fafnir symbolizes the martyrdom of all animals tortured and abused and murdered to "advance" human purposes. The moral is that humankind must cease its mindless, selfish assault on the natural world. Stevie illustrates the poem with a drawing of a knight with a sword. The face is a young woman's, her hair is long, and she is wearing a stylish modern hat: Stevie does not absolve herself from culpability.

Stevie has fun with "The Jungle Husband." He writes a letter to his wife at home:

> Dearest Evelyn, I often think of you
> Out with the guns in the jungle stew
> Yesterday I hittapotamus
> I put the measurements down for you but they got lost in the fuss.
>
> (NW, 35)

The implications are that Evelyn's husband is a foolish, insensitive, and somewhat incompetent man, not likely to survive his jungle adventure. He would have been wiser to have remained at home with his wife.

The often absurd and ludicrous female-male relationship continues to be a theme in the Stevie Smith canon. Besides Evelyn and her hunter husband there are the odd newlyweds in "I Remember," a poem based on Stevie's reading of the autobiography of Littleton Powys, in which he describes his wedding night.[8] It is a dotty delight full of incongruities: an old groom and a young bride who happens to have tuberculosis, the German planes bombing London being passed by the British planes on their way to raid Germany, passionate exclamations and bomb thuds:

> It was my bridal night I remember,
> An old man of seventy-three
> I lay with my young bride in my arms,
> A girl with t.b.
> It was wartime, and overhead
> The Germans were making a particularly heavy raid on Hampstead.
>
> (NW, 38)

Not surprisingly, the young bride is worried about the bombs, but the groom is undeterred: "Harry, do they ever collide? / I do not think it has ever happened, / Oh my bride, my bride" (NW, 38). Like "Not Waving but Drowning," "I Remember" is unforgettable Stevie Smith.

Stevie continue her mild Irish bashing in *Not Waving but Drowning* with "The Celts":

> I think of the Celts as rather a whining lady
> Who was beautiful once but is not so much so now
> She is not very loving, but there is one thing she loves
> It is her grievance which she hugs and takes out walking.
>
> . . . .
>
> The Celtic lady is not very widely popular
> But the English love her oh they love her very much
> Especially when the Celtic lady is Irish they love her
> Which is odd as she hates them then more than anyone else.
>
> (*NW*, 49).

Stevie is easier on the Scots and the Welsh in the poem. Her political conservatism found it difficult to accept the idea that the Irish preferred independence to a benign and enlightened English occupation.

Stevie satirizes the British middle class again in "Parents," who "send their children to public schools" but "who barely can afford it," foolishly attempting to maintain social status when the schools turn the child into a "Happy Fool" (*NW*, 54).

In "The Sorrowful Girl" Muriel rejects her suitor's importuning:

> Muriel, Muriel, marry me Muriel,
> And I will comfort you as well
> And bring life to your pale hair
> And your languid air.
>
> Ah then I shall not be I, for I am here
> With my languid air and lifeless hair
> And I do not feel cold or heat
> I am imprisoned and do not need to be freed
> My prison is my sorrowful mind
> And I do not wish to leave it behind
> Wake me not, leave me here, leave me alone
> I am as God made me, a sorrowful one.
>
> (*NW*, 73)

To save face her lover pretends "he only wanted to marry her for her money." It is hard for him to accept that a girl could find herself beautiful in her solitary sadness and be content with the solace of her mind.

In *Not Waving but Drowning* Stevie continues to evidence her concern for her muse, and she continues to attack insensitive, obsolete critics and poetasters. "The Fairy Bell" has a renegade poet, now a journalist, kill his muse. The woman persona as poet asks in "Who is this Who Howls and Mutters?" Just who is trying to communicate? It is the misunderstood and mistreated "Muse, each word she utters / Is thrown against a shuttered door / And very soon she'll speak no more" (*NW*, 65). Stevie wants her muse to "cry louder," get more attention, and not desert her. Writing is, after all, a soothing balm for the pain of loneliness.

Stevie attacks literary puffery in "The Choosers" by satirizing the fashionable critics who select the "young-man Author of the Month of May." The choosers really "stand in the way" of art and often reject a writer because they "do not like his hat or his Ma." Stevie concludes with a question and an angry answer:

> Oh why does England cherish her arts in this wise,
> Picking inferiorly with grafted eyes?
> It is because it is like the school they never forget,
> So-and-so must be the driven out one, this the pet.
>
> (*NW*, 71)

The philosophical voice in *Not Waving but Drowning* is even stronger than before. As ever, Stevie is ambivalent as to the existence of God. Sometimes she expresses doubt, rejecting Christianity and its cruel "fairy tales." Other times she putatively discusses a deity who is gentle and loving and quite willing to engage in dialogue with her. Stevie the philosopher is calm, detached, and balanced in her observations.

In "King Hamlet's Ghost" Stevie allegorizes loneliness so that old King Hamlet's misery—he is unable to speak unless spoken to—represents all lonely people unable to communicate. The dove of peace in "The Old Sweet Dove of Wiveton" also grieves in loneliness. He sits in his nest, above a world of "retriever dogs in their pursuit," and mourns:

> Murmuring solitary
> Crying for pain,
> Crying most melancholy
> Again and again.
>
> (*NW*, 61)

The old dove is the Christ-like symbol of both human suffering and Christian love.

Stevie emphasizes her role as truth sayer as she plays with a phrase from the *Book of Esdras* in "Magna est Veritas": "Although I collect facts I do not always know what they amount to. / I regard them as a contribution to almighty Truth, magna est veritas et praevalebit, / Agreeing with that Latin writer, Great is Truth and will prevail in a bit" (*NW*, 67). The truth will prevail, but not necessarily right away, nor everywhere, and thus the melancholy of the ironic prophet.

"Anger's Freeing Power" shows how anger can be both a catharsis for the thinker and an energizing force that can knock down barriers. Controlled anger is expressed by the philosophical persona in "But Murderous" as she castigates a mother who

> . . . slew her unborn babe
> . . . .
> Because she did not wish him to be born in a world
> Of murder and war and hate
> "Oh why should I bear a babe from my womb
> To be broke in pieces by the hydrogen bomb?"
>
> (*NW*, 38)

The persona narrator has little pity for the "arrogance of a half-baked mind":

> I say this woman deserves little pity
> That she was a fool and a murderess
> Is a child's destiny to be contained by a mind
> That signals only a lady in distress?
>
> And why should human infancy be so superior
> As to be too good to be born in this world?
> Did she think it was an angel or a baa-lamb
> That lay in her belly furled?
>
> (*NW*, 38)

The mother's little learning is a dangerous thing. The mind must control the heart. Stevie is as hard and firm in her moral convictions as any stoic philosopher.

"The Past" is a perfect clerihew:

> People who are always praising the past
> And especially the times of faith as best
> Ought to go and live in the Middle Ages
> And be burnt at the stake as witches and sages.
>   (*NW*, 62)

A wrong idea is a wrong idea and Stevie makes no bones about it.

Stevie is a searcher. She wants to know the "whys" of life, She struggles to understand, to find reasons, causes, explanations, and she does so fully appreciating the Wittgensteinian handicap: language obfuscates rather than clarifies philosophical questions. In the twentieth century the true poet, striving to communicate feelings and ideas, suffers great frustration and existential angst.

In "Can it Be" the philosophical persona sees a cat hesitate and then make a heroic leap over a lily tank even though she could have walked around. The persona ponders:

> Can it be, can it be
> That beasts are of various bravery
> Some brave by nature, some not at all,
> Some trying to be against a fall?
>   (*NW*, 60)

It is difficult, perhaps impossible, to understand animals, who indeed may take some "thought . . . to cast themselves aloft." How much more difficult then, to understand humans.

Two short, matched poems again underscore Stevie's continuing religious ambivalence: "I. An Agnostic (of his religious friend)" and "II. A Religious Man (of his agnostic friend)." The personae are really the two ever-debating voices in Stevie. The agnostic laughs at his religious friend who "sees quite plain what is not there" but he is kind in his summation because friendship and caring are more important than abstract convictions. The religious man scoffs at the agnostic's views but he shares with his friend the identical, humane closing couplet: "And yet he is more gracious than I, / He has such a gracious personality" (*NW*, 46).

In "The New Age" Stevie despairs of the failures of humankind. The sound of a "New Age coming" will be:

> A sound of drubbing and sobbing
> Of people crying, We are old, we are old
> And the sun is going down and becoming cold
> Oh sinful and sad and the last of our kind
> If we turn to God now do you think He will mind?
>
> (*NW*, 17)

So what if humankind is lost? Humans are not special to creation, no matter what they think: "Oh heavens how these crying people spoil the beautiful geologic scene."

In "A Dream of Comparison" Mary and Eve walk by a river bank where "they talk philosophically." Again Stevie has bifurcated herself into a feeling and a thinking person. Eve, depressed, wishes "to be Nothing." She desire a "cessation of consciousness / With no more impressions beating in / Or various experiences" (*NW*, 22). Mary admonishes her: " 'How can Something envisage Nothing?' said Mary, / 'Where's your philosophy gone?' " (*NW*, 12). The two women "talked until nightfall, / But the difference between them was radical" (*NW*, 22). Mary loves life. Eve wants to "storm back through the gates of Birth." There is no compromise possible. The philosophical persona, simultaneously a Mary and an Eve, is torn apart.

Stevie expresses her conservative pique at the "clergy of the Church of England / Who are always altering the words of the prayers in the Prayer Book" in the poem, "Why are the Clergy . . . ?" She attacks reform and modernization on both theological and aesthetic grounds: "is it not offensive to the ear and also ludicrous?" (*NW*, 37). Although Stevie frequently assaults Christianity, Anglicanism, and Roman Catholicism, she does not want to see the beautiful, historical, moving ceremonies altered.

A perennial question in Stevie's work is "Will Man Ever Face Fact and not Feel Flat?" The "fact" is that humans will never know with certainty if God exists. Stevie is an agnostic with a religious temperament. Christianity is difficult for her to accept, but it is, nevertheless, exciting and stimulating, whereas agnosticism is a bore. Humans "invent fairy stories about everything." God's answer to the human enigma is simply that Man must love or "For lack of love he'll die" (*NW*, 41). But that answer cannot satisfy Stevie. After all, what does God really know about life? Stevie's position is that "Gods don't have to commit themselves—they need not marry, they never sin, they are invariably adequate."[9] In other words, they're not human.

"The Airy Christ" is a simple artist: "For he does not wish that men should love him more than anything / Because he died; he only wishes they would hear him sing (*NW*, 45).

As for humans, in "The Passing Cloud" they are merely the "dust of Continuous Creation." It suffices that "That merry dust does jig so" (NW, 51). One of the most charming and moving poems in Not Waving but Drowning, "In the Park," comes closest of all to dramatizing the spirit of the collection. In it two old men are walking and talking "by the silver lake mid-pooled black in winter." One friend compassionately cries: "Pray for the Mute who have no word to say." They suffer because their "weak thoughts beating in the brain / Generate a sort of heat." The other gentleman, who is nearly deaf, however, proceeds to praise the "newt." Finally, with the aid of a hearing trumpet, they straighten out their garbled communication: "So two, better than one, finally strike truth in this happy song: / 'Praise,' cries the weeping softened one, 'Not pray, praise, all men, / Praise is the best prayer, the least self's there'" (NW, 69). This fine and humble thought is the most pointed sign of maturation and acceptance of life's painful limitations by the three voices of the Stevie Smith canon.

Harold's Leap and Not Waving but Drowning represent the high water mark of Stevie's career as a poet, and the water never receded far. She had discovered and perfected a brilliant method of portraying a genuine malaise while simultaneously assuaging it through her, and thus our, concentration on intense, splenetic, tragicomic vision and precise language.

Chapter Six
"Royal Girls and Royal Times": Poems of the 1960s

The 1960s saw the triumph of Stevie Smith. Her work won the attention and admiration of such diverse poets as Philip Larkin, Robert Lowell, John Betjeman, Roy Fuller, Day Lewis, and Ogden Nash. An enthusiastic American audience developed after *Selected Poems* was published in the United States in 1964. Stevie became a star performer on the poetry circuit, and she won national awards.

On the other hand, her aunt sickened and died, and her own health declined. Stevie's poetry in the 1960s evolved along predictably ambivalent paths. The three-voiced persona in her poetry further matured and her work darkened slightly. The sense of isolation grew, she evidenced more discomfiture with Christian commitment, and thus her poems grew sadder. However, the agon between the sexes waned, even though frustration and disenchantment continued to find expression. Symbolically and paradoxically, the poems show growing self-confidence and security, satisfaction with solitude, and a developing sense of peace and reconciliation with the world.

Stevie's 1960s poetry demonstrates her struggle for self-knowledge and understanding as well as for artistic control and refinement. There is less need to end with nervous giggles a poem that begins on a profound theme, and there are considerably fewer examples of look-at-cute-little-innocent-me-ism. Stevie is now more philosopher than pundit. The cartoonist has waned; her drawings are now less pertinent, seldom complementing the text. She continues, nevertheless, to herald death: to advertise, recommend, and sell it.

Selected Poems

The opportunity to publish her *Selected Poems* (1962), given to her by Longmans, Green, allowed Stevie at the age of sixty to look back on some thirty-five years of writing poetry. She wanted to offer new poems along with those previously published pieces she felt had special merit. The message was that she was still an active poet, producing first-rate work. *Selected Poems* contains 113 poems, fifteen of which appear there for the first time in book form. The new poems in the collection are primarily philosophical and religious expressions, although the lonely, cynical woman persona remains in focus, while the voice of the child persona has faded into the background. Significantly, the first new poem in *Selected Poems* is about writing poetry. "Thoughts about the Person from Porlock" is a highly regarded poem in which Stevie restates the famous Coleridge story of how he was interrupted when writing "Kubla Khan" by a person from Porlock and was never able to recapture the creative moment and complete the poem. Then Stevie accuses Coleridge of having been "stuck with Kubla Khan":

> He was weeping and wailing: I am finished, finished,
> I shall never write another word of it,
> When along comes the Person from Porlock
> And takes the blame for it.[1]

For Stevie, Coleridge uses the person as an excuse. Lonely in her life and work, she longs for a Person from Porlock "To bring my thoughts to an end." The Person represents distraction, company, even death: anything to alleviate depression.

The "One Above" is criticized for experimenting with human character, making the world interesting for the deity "but not for us." God and poets create and compete. Of course God wins, but what can a poet do? Finally, however, Stevie bucks up: "Smile, smile, and get some work to do" (*SP,* 3). In "My Muse" the poet persona pays attention to her muse only when she is unhappy and dissatisfied. "When I am happy I live and despise writing" (*SP,* 120).

Much of Stevie's poetry of the 1960s is strongly antireligious. She wrestles with theology again in "Thoughts about the Christian Doctrine of Eternal Hell," arguing that:

> The religion of Christianity
> Is mixed of sweetness and cruelty
> Reject this Sweetness, for she wears
> A smoky dress out of hell fires
> (*SP,* 4).

The "Christian religion" created God. "Out with him, out with him, let him go" (*SP,* 5). Stevie cannot abide the doctrine of eternal punishment. If God is human-made then hell must be too, and neither is real.

In "Was He Married?" Stevie shifts her attack from Christianity to Christ Himself. He is a false creation of intellectually blinded people: "A god is Man's doll, you ass, / He makes him up like this on purpose" (*SP*, 8). Humans can do better: "A larger one will be when men / Love love and hate hate" (*SP*, 8). And they will do better. Our next God will be greater. Here is Stevie's Teilhardian connection: Stevie hopes for and believes in the perfectability of humankind as we progress toward a final spiritual unity.

The attack on Christianity resumes in "Was it not curious?" Stevie incorrectly attributes Pope Gregory's famous remark on seeing young, fair-haired English (Angles) captives in Rome, "Non Angli sed angeli" ("not Angles but angels"), to Saint Augustine of Canterbury: "Was it not curious of Augustin, Saint Augustin, / When he saw the beautiful British children / To say such a curious thing?" (*SP*, 9). What is curious is that

> He said he must send the gospel, the gospel,
> At once to them over the waves
> He never said he thought it was wicked
> To steal them away for slaves.
> (*SP*, 9)

It is wicked to be more concerned with conversion than with the evils of kidnapping and slavery. The Church's values and perspective are all wrong.

On the other hand Stevie extols Anglican archbishop Cranmer, the old martyr and author of the Anglican Prayer Book, in "Admire Cranmer!" Significantly, she admires Cranmer because of his poetic genius, not his suffering. In "I Was so Full . . ." the persona solipsistically tries to create a Manichaean universe.

> I was so full of love and joy
> There was not enough people to love,
> So I said: Let there be God,
> Then there was God above.
>
> I was so full of anger and hate
> To be hated was not enough people,
> So I said: Let there be a Devil to hate,
> Then down below was the Devil.
> (*SP*, 19)

But then her common sense triumphs. God, religion, and philosophical systems are fairy tales: "So now I say: Away with them, away; we should / Not believe fairy stories if we wish to be good" (*SP,* 19). Stevie likes to turn the universe upside down or inside out in her poetry, placing herself at the center. It may not be humble but it is what all of us really do, after all, in our perceptions of life.

God counterattacks in "God Speaks," but Stevie's God is a humane, rational being, not disposed to such abominations as requiring human sacrifice:

> I made Man with too many faults. Yet I love him.
> And if he wishes, I have a home above for him.
> I should like him to be happy. I am genial.
> He should not paint me as if I were abominable.
> As for instance, that I had a son and gave him for their salvation
> (*SP,* 23).

Furthermore, humans must make their own heaven as they have surely made their own hell. God says: "I should like him to be happy in heaven here, / But he cannot come by wishing. Only by being already at home here" (*SP,* 23). God has plans for us and we must help by cleansing ourselves of superstition and myth. We must grow better and more tolerant of each other's limitations and shortcomings, as implied in "Recognition not Enough": "Sin recognized—but that—may keep us humble, / But oh, it keeps us nasty" (*SP,* 5).

A visit to "Edmonton, thy cemetery . . ." at first depresses the philosophical persona:

> Edmonton, thy cemetery
> In which I love to tread
> Has roused in me a dreary thought
> For all the countless dead,
> Ah me, the countless dead.
> (*SP,* 71)

But then the mood swings to a Wordsworthian optimism:

> Yet I believe that one is one
> And shall for ever be,
> And while I hold to this belief
> I walk, oh cemetery,
> Thy footpaths happily.

>And I believe that two and two
>Are but an earthly sum
>Whose totalling has no part at all
>In heavenly kingdom-come,
>I love the dead, I cry, I love
>Each happy happy one.
>
>　　　　　　　(*SP,* 71)

Here the persona is the solitary woman rejoicing in her independence. That persona, however, is always ambivalent and sometimes manic, for soon "Doubt returns with dreary face / And fills my heart with dread" (*SP,* 71). The persona is left feeling "As if Belief had never been / Ah me, the countless dead, ah me / The countless countless dead" (*SP,* 71). Atypically, Stevie grieves over mortality and is overwhelmed by the sheer enormity of death and, consequently, the improbability of individual salvation.

On a different note, "The Frozen Lake" is a story poem about unrequited love. The witch daughter of the lord of Ullan lives in the lake where Sir Bedevere "Consigned Excalibur." The speaker, a man in love with the witch, throws himself into the lake but finds only the sword of King Arthur as he drowns:

>And so I died, and the lake-water
>That holds the form of Ullan's daughter
>With all my blood is dyed,
>Is dyed,
>With all my love is dyed.
>
>　　　　　　　(*SP,* 12)

In the lovely and graceful "Votaries of Both Sexes Cry First to Venus" the persona again compares love to dying, a lover to Death:

>I love this love; it is eerie if there is not
>My love in my arms then. It is an excitement
>In the arms of a person. It is exciting then,
>It is such an excitement as is on the approach
>Of Death.
>
>　　　　　　　(*SP,* 17)

This time, however, God is kind and "Yes this time when they sang their song they were blessed" (*SP,* 17).

The new poems in *Selected Poems* are about religion, God, the Church, love, and dying. Stevie's subjects basically remain constant, but these pieces are almost without exception some of her most thoughtful and skillful works.

The Frog Prince and Other Poems

The Frog Prince (1966) contains 156 poems, of which sixty-nine appear for the first time in book form. The remainder are poems from the earlier volumes of poetry. The retrospective covers thirty years of work. Stevie was introducing her past efforts to her large new audience, as well as reintroducing the poetry of the earlier decades to her loyal core of followers.

The new poems are nostalgic and recollective, critical of human purpose, and often melancholy. Stevie reverts to the frequent use of the story-poem. Most significantly, she continues her dialogue with the God whose existence she doubts. The sublimation of the child persona voice into reflective pieces on animals is completed in this collection.

The title piece is the most famous Stevie Smith poem after "Not Waving but Drowning." Once more Stevie presents an unexpected perspective on a fairy tale. It is the snail's-eye view, the minor player's prospect, as in Tom Stoppard's *Rosencrantz and Guildenstern Are Dead*. This frog is a nervous animal. He wonders if generally "other enchanted people feel as nervous / As I do?" He thinks of himself as a person despite his amphibian body, and he considers that he has

> . . . been a frog now
> For a hundred years
> And in all this time
> I have not shed many tears.[2]

He is a disenchanted enchanted, but who wouldn't be after a spell of a hundred years? The prince is basically content as a frog:

> I am happy, I like the life,
> Can swim for many a mile
> (When I have hopped to the river)
> And am for ever agile.
>
> And the quietness,
> Yes, I like to be quiet

> I am habituated
> To a quiet life.
>
> (*FP*, 2)

Earthly happiness, however, is no goal for man or beast. Happiness "is part of the spell." One needs ecstasy, so he cries out:

> Come, then, royal girl and royal times,
> Come quickly,
> I can be happy until you come
> But I cannot be heavenly,
> Only disenchanted people
> Can be heavenly.
>
> (*FP*, 2)

"The Frog Prince" is a philosophical poem concerned with the need for transcending those fears and notions that bind us to this safe illusion of a world, for salvation and rebirth follow disenchantment. In the fairy tale the price of self-fulfillment is always a breaking through the chrysalis, a shedding of the old form—a princess emerging from Cinderella's rags. The result, as in heaven, is a fresh, new innocence.

In Stevie's third most famous poem, "The Best Beast of the Fat-Stock Show at Earls Court," her heart is once more wrenched by the suffering of animals. Here the beast is a bull or steer who has won a competition. The poem is written entirely in monosyllables, as if Stevie is somehow trying to speak to, as well as about, the hot and frightened animal:

> When he lay in his pen,
> In the close heat,
> His head lolled, his eyes
> Were not shut for sleep.
>
> (*FP*, 8)

The Best Beast is led away, perhaps to slaughter, even though in a sense he is a king or god:

> Is he not fat?
> Is he not fit?
> Now in a crown he walks
> To the lift.
>
> (*FP*, 8)

A symbol of power and natural majesty, he is to be sacrificed: "Slam the lift door, / Push it up with a groan, / Will they kill the Beast now?" (*FP,* 8). The beast seems aware of his fate just as the persona knows the source of his power:

> I touched his side,
> I touched the root of his horns;
> The breath of the Beast
> Came in low moans.
>
> (*FP,* 8)

The poignancy, sensitivity, compassion, and rhetorical skill of the "The Best Beast" certify it, along with "Not Waving but Drowning" and "The Frog Prince," as a major short English poem of the twentieth century.

"'The Persian' " is a cat named Agnes, the same as the brand of a gas stove that, like the cat, is warm and friendly to the lonely-looking woman in the accompanying illustration. She is cuddling "Agnes." Pets are dependable, and the implication is that humans are not. Agnes will always be there to reflect and share a mood and to give comfort. "Monsieur Pussy-Cat, blackmailer" is a macaronic poem, part French and part English. The persona warns her comfortable cat, "Take care you don't *pousser trop* / The one who gives you such *jolis plats*" (*FP,* 30).

In "Avondall" the woman persona has dreamed she "was a bird / A bird of Avondall." In other words, a suburban bird like herself. She desired "To swoop and swing and call" with other birds. Alas, "no bird turned to me in love / All were inimical, / They were inimical" (*FP,* 43). The persona is unable to "connect" with those who share her environment.

When the lonely, cynical woman persona as "The Listener" hears a radio program about "an encounter with mosquitoes in New Guinea" she "fell to thinking of the animal kingdom / And experienced at once a relief of nervous tension" (*FP,* 48). The animals' battles "are no different from our own," and thus a realization of our solidarity with the beasts brings peace.

"Hymn to the Seal"—a song set to the tune "Soldiers of Christ, arise!"—parodies evangelical music by praising the beautiful seal as a "Creature of God" (*FP,* 49). It is illustrated with a girl holding a tambourine. Is she "beating the drum" for the beasts?

"Fish, Fish" waits, like Moby Dick, for the persona, to take her down to the depths, to his deep world, and to death:

> He is waiting for me
> To carry me to the sea
> I shall be happy then
> In the watery company of his kingdom.
>
> (*FP,* 50)

A woman and a bull again relate in "The Dedicated Dancing Bull and the Water Maid." This time the point of view is the animal's. He wishes he "could be rid of the Water Maid / Or hide from her," for he is much taken with himself:

> Ho ho, thump thump,
> Oh I am elegant, oh I am plump,
> As I wave my head my feet go thud
> On the baked grass. Oh I am good.
>
> (*FP,* 61)

The bull does not wish to dance with the girl, and he does not care if she appreciates his dance. When the night comes he can be a true animal again and go "to the forest pool / And drink and do not think I am a fool" (*FP,* 62). Stevie hates for animals to be trained to entertain humans, and she believes that in their own way, like slaves, they despise us for what we make them do.

"Pretty" is defined by Stevie as what is natural in the world as she uses the opportunity of the poem to show her regard for pike, water rats, otters, beavers, and owls. The human being comes along "like a thief" and steals a look. It is best to "be delivered from humanity / This is prettiest of all, it is very pretty" (*FP,* 67). The misanthropic persona prefers a world without people. Stevie illustrates the poem with a picture of a girl in a large Stevie hat holding an uncomfortable pet on her lap.

"Friends of the River Trent" deplores the pollution in the river. Stevie sardonically ends her "speech" with:

> Then three cheers for the ageing fish, my boys,
> Content in polluted depths
> To grub up enough food, my boys,
> To carry 'em to a natural death,
> And may we do the same, my boys,
> And carry us to a natural death.
>
> (*FP,* 69)

Even more bitingly antipeople is "I am a girl who loves to Shoot." There the persona claims to love animals: "I love the feathered fowl and brute, / I love them with a love as strong / As ever there came from heaven down" (*FP,* 93). Her nonhunting friends doubt her sincerity, but she claims she hunts only when she is hungry, like a predatory animal. She feels "no contradiction or contriteness." Rather, "I love them living and I love them dead with a quick blood spurt / And I may put them in the pot and eat them up with a loving heart" (*FP,* 94). The hunting woman is unable to understand how cruel her murderous actions are, and how most intelligent and sensitive people view her "sport."

Again a woman and a cat find happiness together in "Nodding."

> Tizdal my beautiful cat
> Lies on the old rag mat
> In front of the kitchen fire.
> Outside the night is black.
> The great fat cat
> Lies with his paws under him
> His whiskers twitch in a dream,
> He is slumbering.
>
> (*FP,* 97)

The persona and animal fit together while "creation . . . / Pays for its long plodding / Simply by coming to this— / Cat, night, fire—and a girl nodding" (*FP,* 98). This lovely poem creates the atmosphere of a contented pair in the easiest and best of relations, residing happily in a warm, cozy home.

One poem, "To Carry the Child," shows how costly it is for the poet to maintain the eye and voice of innocent childhood: "The child in adult life is defenceless / And if he is grown-up, knows it" (*FP,* 32). Yet the great value of the child's eye for the poet is that "the child has colours and the man sees no / colours or anything." But still it is desperate and terrible to be both child and adult:

> But oh the poor child, the poor child, what can he do,
> Trapped in a grown-up carapace,
> But peer outside of his prison room
> With the eye of an anarchist?
>
> (*FP,* 33)

Several of the poems in *The Frog Prince* are nakedly autobiographical. "A House of Mercy" is an unabashed recounting of Stevie's childhood in "a house of female habitation" in Palmers Green, and "Avondale," the name of her street, is a sweet, nostalgic recollection of her youth when

> The boys and girls of Avondale
> Do swoop and swing and call,
>
> And all the little cats and dogs,
> Of Avondale, of Avondale,
> In their own way in Avondale
> Do swoop and swing and call,
>
> And oh it is a pleasant sight
> It is a very pleasant sight
> To see the creatures so delight
> To swoop and swing and call,
> In Avondale, in Avondale,
> To see them swoop and call.
>
> (*FP,* 42)

The poem is accompanied by a poignant illustration: a little girl is walking with an older woman whose face is turned away and who is carrying a shopping bag. They are holding hands and the girl is looking back.

"The Small Lady" is illustrated with Stevie as a witch again riding her broomstick at night with her cat on back. The poem's persona is wedded to her "mighty washing machine" and the domesticity it implies. A witch, "passing on the air," tempts the housewoman to escape by joining the freer animal world as a "white duck with a yellow beak." At first the small lady scorns the witch and defends her washing machine: "Human inventions help properly, magic is a disgrace" (*FP,* 68). But quickly the persona cries: "I smell water" and follows the witch "into the setting sun" to freedom. The final, ironic couplet completes the sharp satire: "Heart of my heart, it is a mournful song / Never will this poor lady come home" (*FP,* 68).

The new pieces in *The Frog Prince* include a larger number of long story-poems than in any of Stevie's earlier collections. "I Had a Dream . . ." finds the persona dreaming that she is Helen of Troy. The poem is a remarkable combination of the spirit of the *Iliad* and a modern cynical sensibility. A psychological filter renders the ancient stereotype into contemporary humans. The poem contains a profound and shocking thought. Helen says to Hector:

Well, you know what the Trojan Women
Are going to say about the sack of Troy and being led away
Into captivity, they are going to say: If these things
Had not happened to us we should not be remembered
                                                                    (FP, 18).

Is Helen insensitive or unconscionably cynical or brilliantly intuitive? Is the
possibility of immortality so enticing as to be worth beatings, rape, the death
of husbands and sons, and a life of slavery? Can the implication be that
women never have had any other means of achieving lasting recognition except as victims, martyrs or sacrifices? Or is Helen's voice really that of the romantic poet, convinced that the pain and poverty of a life dedicated to art is a
cheap price for posthumous fame? From time to time the cynical and lonely
woman persona longs to be the beautiful temptress and the cause of discomfiture for men, as in "Die Lorelei." In truth, however, she often settles for Lorelei Lee, but with a guilty conscience.

In her version of "Phèdre" Stevie has Theseus die ("Well, he was old") so
that everything might be "respectable" (FP, 23). There is more than a touch
of the bourgeois in Stevie, longing for the happy ending.

"The Last Turn of the Screw" is based on Henry James's ghost story *The
Turn of the Screw*. Stevie focuses on the relationship between the governess
and Miles. The woman is unaware that she loves her ward. The bright boy
knows she loves him but he does not love her. Stevie's Miles does not die; he is
taken by the evil ghost, Quint, through a rite of passage to maturity and sexual knowledge:

I am Miles, I did not die,
I only turn, as on shut eye
To feel again the silken dress
Of my lost and lovely governess
                                        (FP, 39).

"Widowhood or the Home-Coming of Lady Ross" tells the story of a rich
widow remembering her husband and their peripatetic life. In the end she
wonders: "Oh Harold, our house looks so beautiful today, / Why did you always want to go away?" (FP, 57).

"Is it Happy" reads like an Evelyn Waugh novel. It is the story of a young
aristocrat, son of a field marshal, who struggles in vain to find happiness by
marrying, by converting to Roman Catholicism, and by driving his widowed
mother mad. "Watchful" is a love story, set on the Northumbrian moor, in

which a young girl finds sexual fulfillment by running from home into the woods at night to meet her lover. "The Story I Have Told" is a ghostly fairy tale, and "The Crown of Gold" is a cryptic, allegorical story of a boy searching for security in the form of wealth, not human affection.

The dialogue with death is somewhat abated in the new poems of *The Frog Prince,* but nevertheless it continues. In "Exeat" Stevie tells of a cruel Roman emperor who visits his miserable prisoners in their cells, and when they beg for death, sadistically replies, "Oh no, oh no, we are not yet friends enough. / He meant they were not yet friends enough for him to give them death" (*FP,* 9). Stevie equates her muse with the emperor: "So I fancy my Muse says, when I wish to die, / Oh no, oh no, we are not yet friends enough" (*FP,* 9). Life, however, may come as a lover to "a poet or any person" though he has grown "feeble now and expensive to his country," and life, being easier and kinder than the muse, may allow the poet or any person to commit suicide. It is life who gives us to death if it has grown to love us. Stevie never was more direct in stating her feelings about suicide than in "Exeat." Better swift, self-imposed death than enfeeblement and dependency, Stevie's greatest fears.

"Oh Christianity, Christianity" is another attack on her religion, particularly the doctrine of incarnation. Christianity seems "a theology of false appearances" and of obscurantism: "Oh what do you mean, what do you mean? / You never answer our questions" (*FP,* 12). However, in the very next poem, "Why do you rage?" the persona castigates herself: "Why do you rage so much against Christ?" But after calling Him "Truth, Beauty, Love, Wonder, Holiness" and trying to "say, Yes" she sadly confesses: "Oh I would if I thought it were so" (*FP,* 13).

In "Dear Child of God," an ironic title, Stevie attacks the diety for creating humankind in the image of Darwin: "You made the terms of our survival / That we should use our intelligence / To kill every rival" (*FP,* 20). Why did God force us through natural selection to become so ferocious? Stevie admonishes God: "It is not often we remember / You put this poison in us" (*FP,* 20). In the end, however, all we can do is stand "With the tears on our face / And our hands clasped in anger, / Faithful but unfortunate" (*FP,* 20).

The couplet "Pearl" is dedicated "To an American lady poet committing suicide because of not being appreciated enough": "Then cried the American poet where she lay supine: / 'My name is Purrel; I was caast before swine' " (*FP,* 54). Here Stevie must have had in mind Sylvia Plath, who committed suicide in 1963. She had expressed her admiration for Stevie Smith in writing a few months before her death.[3] She had also sent Stevie a fan letter with a request that they meet. Stevie replied, but as it turned out there was not enough time.

In "Voices from the Tomb (1)" Stevie writes an epitaph for a poet with a writer's block. In the end being blocked matters little: "Poor Soul, keep silent, in Death's clime / There's no pen, paper, notion, / And no Time" (*FP,* 58). The last of the new poems in *The Frog Prince,* "Some Are Born," is a summary and an envoi as Stevie shrugs off all seriousness:

> Some are born to peace and joy
> And some are born to sorrow
> But only for a day as we
> Shall not be here tomorrow.
>   (*FP,* 107)

The Best Beast

The American edition of *Selected Poems,* published by New Directions in 1964, had been a success, and Stevie's popularity on this side of the Atlantic was growing through acceptance of her poems in U.S. periodicals, when Alfred A. Knopf negotiated with Longmans for the publication of a collection of forty-four poems to be titled *The Best Beast* (1969). Only seven of these had not been published previously in book form and six of the seven would be reprinted in the posthumous *Scorpion and Other Poems* (1972).

"A Soldier Dear to Us" is one of Stevie's most heartfelt and moving poems. It is an in memoriam to a wounded World War I soldier on whom she had a crush when she was twelve.

> Basil never spoke of the trenches, but I
> Saw them always, saw the mud, heard the guns, saw the duckboards,
> Saw the men and the horses slipping into the great mud, saw
> The rain fall and never stop falling, saw the gaunt
> Trees and the rusty frame
> Of the abandoned gun carriages. Because it was the same
> As the poem "Childe Roland to the Dark Tower Came"
> I was reading at school.[4]

As a child as well as a civilian Stevie could not directly know the horrors of trench warfare, but she related it to the unseen horror and dread in Robert Browning's poem. Although Stevie's contact with Basil first occurred over fifty years before she wrote the poem, the memory remains fresh: "Oh Basil, I was a child at school, / My school lessons coloured / My thoughts of you" (*BB,* 13). In the "envoi" Stevie reveals that:

Now fifty years later
Basil has died of the shots he got in the shell crater
The shrapnel has worked round at last to his merry heart, I write this
For a memorial of the soldier dear to us he was.

(*BB*, 13).

The schoolgirl patriot and the caring woman are also there, down deep in the many-voiced persona of the Stevie Smith canon.

"The House of Over-Dew," one of Stevie's longest poems, is the story of the fate of a middle-class family that leaves the suburbs to buy and run a retreat for missionaries, Over-Dew. The move proves to be a human and financial disaster. The Minnims, "sincere and practicing Christians" (*BB*, 64), come to realize that faith is not enough to sustain them. The family is narrow-minded and mean-spirited, and the persona denigrates them for their mistreatment of their future daughter-in-law. Stevie always values people over principles, and kin over causes. Despite the poetry layout, however, "The House of Over-Dew" is really a prose allegory.

"The Ass" is a fairy-tale poem about Eugenia, "a happy idle ass" who drowns "where the great waves crash," but is happy in death "as if / All her best wish had come to pass" (*BB*, 41). For all living creatures a natural life and a quick death are best.

Another animal poem is "Hippy-Mo." He was "a sweet bird" at first, but "he grew tall as a house" until he "Took me in his claws and would / Not let me go" (*BB*, 52). Like a great eagle he takes the persona "to a sunny land" and puts her "in a cage," where she rages. He holds her hand so tightly she cannot move, and he will not tell her if he wishes her to die. This fascinating poem is a dream of being taken and dominated by a brute and masculine force that is both life and death. The persona is ambivalently thrilled and infuriated by her abduction and incarceration.

"O Pug" is ostensibly about her friends Anna and Michael Browne's dog, but is really about Stevie's insecurity after the death of her aunt. She begins with a justification: "O Pug, some people do like you" and ends with a call for understanding and compassion:

O Pug, obstinate old nervous breakdown,
In the midst of so much love,
And such comfort,
Still to feel unsafe and be afraid,

How one's heart goes out to you!

(*BB*, 88)

Although Stevie was cosseted by her friends, when she lived alone she was afraid of loneliness itself, and she deeply feared the future with its seemingly inevitable physical decline and dependency on others.

The Best Beast is the last book Stevie Smith published in her lifetime. Neither its new poems or those in the posthumous *Scorpion* show any decline in poetic power. The particolored voices and the riposte remain vibrant. Rigidity, cruelty, hypocrisy, and uncompassionate church doctrine are still macerated. Only the child's voice has faded, while the philosopher's has grown to predominance. The satiric element has lessened; the profound element has deepened. Poetry may have become less fun for Stevie, but she was very far from giving it up. It had become her life.

Chapter Seven

"It Might Have Better Been": Last Poems

Stevie Smith's life ended abruptly and relatively early. She was not seriously ill until ten weeks or so before her death at the age of sixty-eight. Stevie wrote poetry almost to her last days. In fact she made her final contribution to *Scorpion* from her hospital bed, and she was concerned about her selections and the fate of the collection to the very end. She was a poet till the stars grew pale. Her friend, the editor James MacGibbon, assembled her monument: *The Collected Poems of Stevie Smith* (1975).

Scorpion and Other Poems

Although she did not know it, Stevie had barely enough time to put *Scorpion* together. It is a slim volume, only thirty-two poems, of which six first appeared in book form in *Best Beast* and one in *Not Waving but Drowning*. Death is the dominant theme in the collection, and much of Stevie's humor and satire has fled. She is alternately splenetic and resigned to fame's ephemerality and life's termination. The burden of this knowledge is almost too heavy to bear.

Stevie sometimes thought of herself as a scorpion, a creature with a sting in its tail.[1] Like "witch" and "The Princess Anemone" it was an appellation she enjoyed and promoted, especially late in her life. However, *Scorpion* does not sting. The persona is often a worn-out and disillusioned old woman like "Mrs Briggs" in the title poem, who thinks that the moment of God's judgment would be like a visit to "the Out-Patients' Department." She is only a stinging insect but she wants so much for God to want her:

> O Lord God please come
> And require the soul of thy Scorpion
>
> Scorpion so wishes to be gone.[2]

Death is a permanent solution to loneliness only if there is a need for her soul "to waft over grass till it comes to the blue sea / I am very found of grass, I always have been." As for people or even animals: "Sea and *grass* must be quite empty / Other souls can find somewhere *else*" (*S*, 1).

"Oh grateful colours, bright looks!" shows Stevie's delight in the small beauties of life, the flowers. She cannot get her fill of them as she enters old age:

> Seize colours quick, heap them up while you can.
> But perhaps it is a false tale that says
> The landscape of the dead
> Is colourless.
>
> (*S*, 35)

Dare she hope that there will be fields and flowers for her soul to wander in after death?

In "Oblivion" life is calling the persona back but oblivion is too sweet. Still there is time: "But I can wait for her, her gentle mist / And those sweet seas that deepen are my destiny / And must come even if not soon" (*S*, 51).

"Black March" extols "a friend" who can provide eventual relief. Stevie teases us:

> I have a friend
> At the end
> Of the world.
> His name is a breath
>
> Of fresh air.
>
> (*S*, 56)

Of course we expect to read "death" instead of "breath." Paradoxically, the end of breathing is both the termination and commencement of existences in this poem. It is "a change for you," whatever that change may be.

In "Grave by a Holm-Oak" the persona questions the interred woman, named Anna, probably Stevie's aunt, Margaret Annie Spear:

> Where have the dead gone?
> Where do they live now?
> Not in the grave, they say,
> Then where now?
>
> (*S*, 57)

The only response comes from a tree and the snow: "Ask not, cries the holm-oak, Weep, says snow" (*S,* 57). Stevie is unsure of an afterlife. Logic can not help her. It doesn't look good. "The Sea-widow" is a remarkable dialogue between a widow and the spirit of her dead husband, who remains jealous. He asks: "Do you wish I was back?" He also wants to know if she is sleeping with someone, and he is shocked when she replies: "A black man comes in with the evening tide." The ghost shouts: "What is his name? Tell me! How does he dare?" The lonely women confesses: "He comes uninvited, His name is Despair" (*S,* 58).

Stevie wrote "The Stroke" for her sister, Molly, who had suffered one and for whom Stevie was caring.[3] The poem concerns a once beautiful plant that is blighted although its heart remains youthful.

In *Scorpion* Stevie's concern for animals merges with and is ineluctably incorporated into her ever-growing accommodation with death. "The Donkey" is a retired beast who "after a lifetime of working . . . was now free to go merrymaking." Yet it is not happy in its freedom. It and the persona know that independent anarchy leads to "Death's odder anarchy" and that "our pattern will be broken all up. / though precious we are momentarily, donkey, / I aspire to be broken up" (*S,* 24). The pattern of the persona has been the image of loneliness, and though there is some value left in her life and work, she is ready for death to break that pattern.

In "Cock-a-Doo" the persona loves "to hear the cock crow in / the middle of the day"; once, twice, each time the sound grows sharper:

> . . . If there were
> A third sharpener
> Coming this hot day with a butcher's edge
> It would spell death.
>
> (*S,* 25)

"The Sallow Bird" is an attempt to re-create a Middle English ballad about a bird lacking love. "Mrs Blow and Her Animals" reverses the usual perspective of humans observing beasts. Her two animal friends, Clanworthy the dog and Hopdance the cat, live together and worry about their mistress's health. "The Galloping Cat" is a happier, funnier poem, reminiscent of the work of the younger Stevie. The cat gallops around "doing good," it thinks. Rather, he is a cat cyclone, attacking even angels, who do not know "What's what and that / Galloping about doing good / Is a full-time job" (*S,* 53).

A masochistic woman is the persona in "Seymour and Chantelle or Un peu de vice." Ostensibly the poem is "in memory of A. Swinburne and Mary

Gordon," but the erotic piece, describing the sadomasochistic relationship
between a young couple, far exceeds Stevie's actual knowledge of the affair
between the poet and his cousin. Stevie's poem is so psychologically true and
so sexually charged that it almost jumps off the page and out of the canon:

> Pull my arm back, Seymour,
> Like the boys do,
> Oh Seymour, the pain, the pain,
> Still more then, do.
>
> (S, 2)

Details of flagellation, implied oral sex, and orgasm emerge from a cascade
of provocative images: "Oh the pain, the pain, / Kiss me and I will kiss you
again." What makes the poem particularly unusual is that Stevie clearly ab-
horred cruelty. Yet even late in life she had a need, at least one time, to high-
light eroticism and paint a vivid picture of perverse sexual pain and pleasure.

The poem immediately following "Seymour and Chantelle," "How do you
see?" quickly, if temporarily, erases the salacious thoughts evoked by the former. Here again Stevie is attacking modern Christian faith. In this essay
poem she feels that the "Holy Spirit of God" as the "Holy Ghost" is beautiful
but only in the context of a fairy tale. She asks theological questions, tries to
answer them, but is dissatisfied with the answers:

> Oh Christianity, Christianity,
> Why do you not answer our difficulties?
> If He was God He was not like us
> He could not lose.
>
> (S, 7)

The fearsome potential result of the intellectual failure of Christianity is appalling:

> I do not think we shall be able to bear much longer the dishonesty
> Of clinging for comfort to beliefs we do not believe in,
> For comfort, and to be comfortably free of the fear
> Of diminishing good, as if truth were a convenience.
> I think if we do not learn quickly, and learn to teach children,
> To be good without enchantment, without the help
> Of beautiful painted fairy stories pretending to be true,
> Then I think it will be too much for us, the dishonesty,

And armed as we are now, we shall kill everybody,
It will be too much for us, we shall kill everybody,

                                                    (*S*, 9)

What tortures Stevie is the impelling intellectual honesty that forces her to look at Christianity through a magnifying glass. Inevitably, she is then shocked at the fragility and imperfections of its mystery.

In "The Forlorn Sea" the cynical woman persona has a fantasy of being invited to the royal wedding of "A fairy King," who then takes his "Princess" back to a palace "By the forlorn sea." There the persona is allowed to play as a pampered child:

> It is like a dream
> When they kiss and cuddle me,
> But I like it, I like it,
> I do not wish to break free.
>   (*S*, 16)

She becomes a lotus eater who will do anything to avoid a return to reality:

> So I eat all they give me
> Because I have read
> If you eat fairy food
> You will never wake up in your own bed.
>   (*S*, 17)

"Angel Bogey" is another slightly versified narrative like "The House of Over-Dew." Based on an infamous murder case, it is the story of a sixteen-year-old wife named "Angel" who poisons her mother and her own husband because they are child murderers. Angel becomes the Angel of Death. Interestingly, Stevie shows great love for children in her poetry, while in life she often felt they were her rivals.

"Francesca in Winter" is a young woman, shown in the arms of a man, who seeks peace instead of sexual passion. She wishes

> . . . hellfire
> Played fire's part
> And burnt to end
> Flesh soul and heart

Then we could sit beside our fire
With quiet love.

(S, 26)

Heaven must intercede and give quietude to creatures driven by nature to the
frenzy of procreation.

The human race feeds on pain in "So to fatness come." The persona
dreams that someone, perhaps Death, will allow her "to sup full of the dish"
he gives her so she may "to fatness come" and "know peace" (S, 27). The cynical woman persona is less cynical now; the striving is for quiescence.

In "Nor We of Her to Him" the persona leaves her own difficulties and
sadness behind to show her concern for a male friend's troubled relationship
with his mate who "eats him day and night / And draws the blood from
him" (S, 32). It is excruciatingly painful to see a friend being destroyed and
not be in a position to give aid. One is often helpless to speak comfort, the
friend is mute in misery, and nothing can be done. Men and women, their
ways and their wars, their sometime truces, and their inevitable incompatibil-
ity are a perduring subject in the lifelong writing of Stevie Smith.

"Archie and Tina" are childhood friends as Stevie reminisces about her
own youth as her days begin to run out. That early period is recollected as a
time of great happiness: "Oh what pleasure, what pleasure!" She wonders.
"Where are you today / Archie and Tina, / Playmates of my childhood"
(S, 39). She wishes that her childhood could be lived again: "Oh, if only; oh
if only!"

The last poem in *Scorpion* is the last Stevie wrote, completing it in the hospital a few weeks before her death.[4] Her longtime friend and, later, literary
executor, James MacGibbon, read "Come Death" (the second poem with
that title) at her funeral service. The persona is ready for death: "I feel ill.
What can the matter be?" The servant death must do his duty: "Listen then
to this sound I make, it is sharp, / Come Death. Do not be slow" (S, 60).

In *Scorpion* Stevie Smith bundles up the iterative themes of her poetry. She
did not do it purposely. It merely happens that the collection satisfactorily
end-stops Stevie's long discourse on Christianity (about which their seems
little more she could add), her need to evoke and examine her childhood and
youth, her love for animals, and her fierce loneliness. Furthermore, she recon-
ciles and blends her poetic voices: the girl child and adolescent; the cynical,
lonely woman; and the skeptical philosopher. The dominant mood of the last
poems swerves away from the evanescence of the earlier volumes and instead
projects a softening, an easing, and a sense of wearied relief like the quiet after
a great storm.

Collected Poems

The Collected Poems of Stevie Smith (1975), carefully and caringly edited and introduced by James MacGibbon, is the bedrock of Stevie's growing reputation as a significant, perhaps major, poetic voice. It contains all the poems of seven previous poetry books and one previously uncollected poem, "Goodnight," as well as an addition to "The Stroke."[5]

"Goodnight," placed last in the collection though it was written in 1938, is vintage Stevie. The cynical woman persona observes her friends, a married couple named Miriam and Horlick who have an affectionate dog named Tuggers. Their marriage is hellish. The dog obviously cares more for his mistress than does Horlick. All are gathered in the guest bedroom where the persona is preparing to go to bed: "Tuggers was the dog. And he was getting excited. So / Miriam had taken her stockings off and you know / Tuggers was getting excited licking her legs, slow, slow" (CP, 572). Horlick is clearly jealous of Tuggers even though he really has no desire left for his wife: "It's funny Tuggers should be so enthusiastic, said Horlick nastily, / It must be nice to be able to get so excited about nothing really, / Try a little higher up old chap, you're acting puppily" (CP, 572). Bored, the persona yawns. The couple say goodnight and leave Miriam "quite white / With sorrow."

The marriages of many of Stevie's friends were negative models for Stevie; "Goodnight" is clearly based on personal observation. In one part of her mind Stevie always believed she had escaped a sorry fate by remaining single.

Me Again

The indefatigable scholar-editors Jack Barbera and William McBrien located sixty-three more of Stevie's poems that either had not been published at all or had appeared in periodicals but were not included in any of her collections. Apparently Stevie did not think these poems worthy of including in her various volumes, but some are truly deserving of critical attention. All, of course, are of interest to lovers of Stevie Smith's poetry. They have been reissued in the anthology Me Again (1981).

"Marriage I think" (1937) is a typically witty attack on that institution.

> Marriage I think
> For women
> Is the best of opiates.
> It kills the thoughts.
> (MA, 216)

The woman in the illustration, wearing a 1930s hat and sitting rather expectantly on a bed, looks much like the author.

"Mother Love" (n.d.) sums up Stevie's view of yet another institution requiring association with men, motherhood:

> Mother love is a mighty benefaction
> The prop of the world and its population
> If mother love died the world would rue it
> No money would bring the women to it.
>
> (*MA*, 217)

"The Octopus" satirizes the relationship between mothers and sons. Mother is ready to smother

> Darling little Tom and Harry,
> When time comes for you to marry
> . . . .
> Mother will be close at hand.
>
> (*MA*, 218)

As for life in nature, the experience of "Henry Wilberforce" suffices:

> Henry Wilberforce as a child
> Was much addicted to the pleasures of the wild;
> He observed Nature, saw, remembered,
> And was by a natural lion dismembered.
>
> (*MA*, 218)

Several of Stevie's previously uncollected poems bash editors and critics (best left out of collections to be reviewed?) including "Tom Snooks the Pundit" (n.d.) who shouts:

> "Down with creative talent
> (I have none)
> Down with creative talent
> Kick it down!"
>
> (*MA*, 225)

"The Old Poet" (n.d.) dying in poverty says: "I'd've done much better as a literurry editor" (*MA*, 226). And "They Killed" (1953) "a poet by neglect / . . . treating him worse than an insect" (*MA*, 227).

"The Holiday" (1961) and "On the Dressing Gown Lent Me by My Hostess the Brazilian Consul in Milan, 1958" (n.d.), like "Goodnight," are satirical poems depicting Stevie's often difficult relationships with friends. The former piece shows that the poet sometimes did not enjoy the weekends away as a house guest that she so frequently sought;

> Say goodbye to the holiday, then,
> To the peace you did not know,
> And to the friends who had power over you,
> Say goodbye and go.
>
> (*MA*, 229)

The "Milan" poem is especially fine, but surely too personal for Stevie to have published it. After all, the persona states she "ran together in the streets" with her hostess's husband and that she stood in the fusillade of words between the married couple. Furthermore, the persona and the husband cried "Give us money . . . you have not given us much." And most shocking of all: "I admit your dressing gown / Wrapped around me from the offences of the town" (*MA*, 247). This amusing autobiographical poem shows a scandalous, hard-drinking, saturnalian side of Stevie not very much evidenced elsewhere in her writing. The poem is a delightfully wicked confession.

Not surprisingly, many of Stevie's strong, previously uncollected poems are about death, including "When I Awake" (1938), "Beautiful" (1957), and "Roaming" (n.d.): "What is belief? / I only know when I speak of Death / I experience relief" (*MA*, 233).

The last poem in *Me Again* is illustrated by a little girl with a smiling face who seems to be saying "I thank thee, Lord" (1969):

> . . . for my beautiful bed
> Have mercy on those who have none
> And may all thy children still happier lie
> When they to thy kingdom come.
>
> (*MA*, 250)

As a romantic poet Stevie, of course, worked out of her life experience. Although she fragmented her persona into three voices—the child and adolescent; the cynical, lonely woman; and the skeptical philosopher—they were all really facets of a diamond talent. She mulched and cultivated her unhappy and sickly early childhood, her tentative adventures in love, her disappointments as a woman in a male-dominated society, the security of her life with her aunt, her loneliness, and the tedium of her secretarial job, in a soil already fertile with genius. There flowered a witty, funny, poignant, critical, and cruel garden of verse. As a philosophical poet Stevie examined everything and accepted nothing on face value. Her song is the nursery rhyme; her fable is the myth and the fairy tale; her language is King James and the *Daily Mirror*. She was and is a twentieth-century poet sui generis.

Chapter Eight
Child and Witch: Achievement and Summation

At the memorial service for Stevie Smith, the eulogist listed the "apparent antinomies" of Stevie's character, "her innocence and sophistication, her compassion and familiarity with the glee of cruelty," all of which caused her to play at one and the same time "the roles of child and witch."[1] These two images, confirmed in her mind, form the double helix from which blew the tornado of her art. That constricted storm danced and still dances across a flat landscape, leaving a stunned and quizzical readership knocked down, and staring after the whirlwind just passed.

Growth

Stevie Smith did not publish her first book until she was thirty-four. Fame then came almost instantly, followed by a gradual decline in reputation to near oblivion. But fame came again when she was in her sixties, and she was a celebrity until she died. Stevie was not a turn-of-the-century man-hater, a New Woman of Edwardian cut, or a protomodernist "no man" woman. She was something of a Victorian, and in many ways as much a Tory as any stuffy club man. She was also a flapper with, as Philip Larkin says, the skittishness and compulsiveness of "a kind of Gertrude Stein—Daisy Ashford—Lorelei Lee."[2] Stevie's childhood, particularly the loss of her father's presence and love, and her long, stable, supportive, symbiotic relationship with her Aunt Margaret formed the foundation of the emotional structure from which she mounted her attack on life, her taunting of God, and her revenge on men.

Development

Although she had written poems long before she attempted fiction, the method of Stevie's great poetry burst out of her technique as a novelist. In that genre she was essentially a monologist, and as a poet the act was the same: singing her biting, silly, sad, funny, tragic, cruel, compassionate, self-

pitying, self-hating songs of herself just as they struck her. Stevie was essentially a doodler. The simpler, monosyllabic words of ordinary conversation
provided the small tiles of her trenchant verses and the device with which she
encoded her ideas and emotions, fusing sound with signification. Stevie
trusted her readers to add appropriate color and connotation to her works as
they decoded them. "Her gift," says Seamus Heaney, "was to create a peculiar
emotional weather between the words."³

The three voices of Stevie's poetic persona—the child and adolescent; the
lonely, cynical woman; and the philosopher—sprang from the novels. As
time passed, the balance and proportion of this triadic persona shifted, so
that, slowly, the voice of the child faded, that of the lonely, cynical woman
grew less strident, and the philosopher, stoical and critically agnostic, came to
dominate. Stevie moved from the cultural subversion of "childishness" to direct confrontation in philosophical debate.

Although, as much as any twentieth-century writer, Stevie has a distinctive
voice, there are obvious influences on her work. She reinvented and decon-
structed the magic folk tale, *die Märchen*, turning them into "fractured fairy
tales." William Blake seems to have been often in her mind. His religious nature, simple language, contrasting visions of heaven and hell, delicate shifts
of stress, shadowy mythologies, and metaphysical gifts find distant echo in
Stevie's verse. Samuel Taylor Coleridge's transcendental wisdom and his
ability to lose himself in dreams and fantasies awed Stevie. Alfred, Lord
Tennyson's narratives and Robert Browning's dramatic soliloquies, all well
studied in her youth, worked on Stevie's mind too. With Emily Dickinson's
life, art, and metaphysic there was clear sympathy and identification. Edward
Lear's trick of juxtaposing humorous verse with illustrations inspired Stevie,
as did James Thurber's technique.

Significantly, Stevie owes no debt to other modern British or American
poets. She was almost pathologically afraid of seeming to fall under their
influences. Consequently she adamantly refused to read them. Living as
she did in near seclusion for most of her life, she insulated herself from the
mainstream and milieu of post–World War II British poetry. Although
Stevie achieved great popularity with the young poetry audience of the
1960s, she was never even remotely considered a Beat poet of the 1950s or
a Rock poet of the next generation. She was almost totally apolitical as artist and citizen, neither stridently antiwar nor anticommunist. Rather, she
was against things, especially noisy things. Poetry mattered to her, not politics. Calvin Bedient says that Stevie "had no view, only views."⁴ She
changed her mind a lot, just like most of the rest of us, but she was very
good at finding the truth in a subject.

In a way, Stevie never forgot her middle-class suburban neighbors as she developed as a writer. Even though she claimed that she did not want them to know about her literary life, she used their vocabulary as she satirized their values, and she seemed always to envision those cursory readers as a large part of her audience, for a great beauty of Stevie's poetry is that one does not have to be a poet or scholar to enjoy it. Although the poetry functions on many levels, it is always accessible.

Feminism

Stevie was not a feminist. She would not have been a suffragist in her mother's generation. She was, of course, a highly intelligent, sensitive woman. Like so many sharp, critical, modern women she longed for men to be fair, kind, gentle, strong, and supportive, while believing that they are generally inadequate, unfeeling, and destructive. Alas, her observations and experiences did not prove her wrong. In the mimetic, miniature world created by her words, she found the control that escaped her in the real world.

Patricia Meyer Spack notes that "the cliché that women, more consistently than men, turn inward for sustenance seems to mean, in practice, that women have richly defined the ways in which imagination creates possibility: possibility that society denies."⁵ Working in and exploited by the inner world of London business, one totally male dominated, Stevie knew that the conventional concept of femininity included a measure of subjugation and service. Not wanting to be a passive women, yet unwilling to seek alliances with other women, Stevie fought the ancient battle against male control alone and in the only way she could: by being herself. Her work was agitprop only for the cause of Stevie.

Death

From childhood on Stevie contemplated, respected, and valued death. As youth and young woman she lived through two suicidal European wars. She "lost" her father and mother early. Her century witnessed the apparent death of the Christian God. What other god was left but Death? That final, faithful deity always kept the key to the door of eternity and oblivion ready for her. It was surely the kinder god.

Stevie, like Dorothy Parker in *Enough Rope* (1926) and *Sunset Gun* (1928), saw death as a lover to be embraced most gladly. Suicide, in extremis, was a sure means of alleviating misery. Unlike Parker, whose infatuation with suicide was always a romantic flirtation, a perpetual adolescent's idée

fixe, Stevie's view of the most desperate act was that it presented an intellectual solution within a stoic philosophy. It was never a reflexive reaction to depression or despair. She did not play Russian roulette. Only once did she try
to use the wild card each player at life is given. Death could wait, and did. For
those who suffer, death is freedom. The pain of loss is ours, the living. Janice
Thaddeus believes that Stevie's "dance macabre is always so vital, death and
life seem to be inextricably mixed, that we leave her feeling braver, able to
laugh at whatever comes our way."[6]

Religion

Stevie left a body of metaphysical poetry the significance of which is still
being plumbed. Stevie saw cruelty and dishonesty in the Church, and although she simultaneously could be believer, agnostic, and even atheist, she
set about reconstructing God, creating a kinder, more sympathetic, less
vengeful deity, a feminine God, while yet allowing Him His maleness. He
could be in charge of the vast universe, but He had better be a loving God.

Thus Stevie rejected the Christian doctrine of heaven and hell. Oblivion
follows death. Hell is humanity. Not all of Stevie's religious poems are
heterodoxical, however. She found drama and excitement in religion. Although she preferred the values and ceremonies of her own Anglican Church,
the Roman Catholic ritual could also move and inspire her. She wanted to believe. Indeed, the Christian religion was beautiful but dangerous for Stevie.
Her emotions flew up to heaven but her thoughts tripped her feet and made
her fall to earth. If man was God's doll, God was man's.

Although Stevie scoffed at the return to religion during World War II, and
in the immediate postwar era the subject was never far from her mind. She
was always willing, indeed eager, to talk about as well as write on religion.
Many of her review assignments were books on religion, and she was not unhappy with those selections. It was as if she were searching for answers she
knew were not to be posited.

Stevie's criticisms of Christianity, besides her vehement disagreement with
the belief in eternal punishment, include disbelief in the story of Creation,
that God would bargain for human redemption with the death of his Son,
that Scripture is divinely inspired, and that the Holy Spirit is the sole source
of the inspiration of good. In the end, if she could not share all the beliefs of
her fellow humans, she could share and even love the humanity behind their
religious drives. In another age Stevie would have been either a holy woman
or a witch. In her own time she found life was sermon enough.

Achievement

Stevie Smith's reputation rests on her three novels and nine volumes of verse. Her poems, made more easily accessible in *Collected Poems*, constitute a distinct body of satiric, cynical, sometimes poignant verse that seems to delineate the role of twentieth-century Western women in transition from chattel to independence. Her poems are nonacademic, flesh-and-blood lyrics that try to define reality rather than seek a transcendental method of escape. They are refreshingly different from the pinched formalism of most of her contemporaries. Her poetry is widely recognized as a major contribution to midcentury literature, and it appears destined for a widening readership, growing admiration, and concomitant study.

Joyce Carol Oates points out that Stevie "is justly celebrated for her remarkable poetry, which magically combines the rhythms of light verse . . . with the unyielding starkness of a tragic vision."[7] In that vision she attempts to redefine Christianity, to help redress the grievances of modern women through satire and sarcasm, to protest the suffering imposed on animals, and to talk to the angels.

Stevie wrote without waste. She sharpened and trimmed. The appearance of garrulousness is just that, an illusion, created by a subsuming naiveté. Rather, she is reductive, rendering to the direct, the truthful, the clear. She is also one of the most musical British poets of the century.

Stevie created her own zoo. It has Blakean overtones. Many of the denizens are unforgettable: the Best Beast, Fafnir the dragon, the noble dog Belvoir, and the various cats, lions eating Christians, birds, donkeys, scorpions, and so on. Usually her animals are naturally good, and they suffer for us as well as because of us. Left to our tender mercies they become martyrs. Like Emily Dickinson, Stevie created her own circumscribed world, one whole and coherent, if slightly tilted; one sculpted by a moralist with compassion. There is more than a touch of expressionism in it, and the colors are often the blacks, grays, and whites of early film.

Stevie Smith was a strong woman and a great artist. She advocated and practiced endurance. She admonished all to be brave and to fulfill life so that we may deserve death. She refused to be "literary" even though she loved words. She had fun with her no-nonsense "nonsense" verse. She could be wicked, tricky, vituperative, and spiteful. In archetypal Jungian terms Stevie's personal myth identification was Hermes, the solitary explorer, the swift traveler, the trickster, the troublemaker, the persuader. Wonderful transformations occur in her poems—a frog becomes a prince, a secretary is sucked up into a Turner seascape—but the greatest of transformations, her own, occurred because of her work. The child-woman from the suburban house of female habitation, forever angered by and grieving over the loss of her father, evolved into a major and unique voice in twentieth-century British poetry.

Notes and References

Chapter One

. Peter Orr, ed. *The Poet Speaks* (London: Routledge & Kegan Paul, 1966), 230.
2. Ibid., 229.
3. Jack Barbera and William McBrien, *Stevie: A Biography of Stevie Smith* (1985; reprint, New York: Oxford University Press, 1987), 9.
4. "A House of Mercy," *The Collected Poems of Stevie Smith* (1975; reprint, New York: Oxford University Press, 1976), 410; hereafter cited in the text as *CP*.
5. Kay Dick, *Ivy and Stevie: Ivy Compton-Burnett and Stevie Smith* (1971; reprint, London: Allison & Busby, 1983), 61, 64–65.
6. Barbera and McBrien, *Stevie*, 29.
7. Dick, *Ivy and Stevie*, 65–66.
8. Ibid., 81.
9. Ibid., 69.
10. Orr, *The Poet Speaks*, 228.
11. Barbera and McBrien, *Stevie*, 44–47.
12. Ibid., 322.
13. Ibid., 56.
14. Dick, *Ivy and Stevie*, 70.
15. *Cats in Colour* (London: Batsford, 1959), 12; hereafter cited in the text as *CC*.
16. Dick, *Ivy and Stevie*, 73.
17. Arnold Palmer, "Winter Flowering Novelists," *Yorkshire Post*, 19 January 1938, 6.
18. Orr, *The Poet Speaks*, 230.
19. Frank Swinnerton, "New Novels," *Observer*, 23 January 1938, 6.
20. George Stonier, "Five Poets, Five Worlds," *New Statesman* 16 (3 December 1938): 930.
21. *Me Again: Uncollected Writings of Stevie Smith*, ed. Jack Barbera and William McBrien (1981; reprint, New York: Farrar, Straus and Giroux, 1982), 272; henceforth cited in the texts as *MF*
22. Barbera and McBrien, *Stevie*, 293.
23. Ibid., 139.
24. Dick, *Ivy and Stevie*, 73.
25. "Women at Work," *Tribune*, 23 September 1949, 20.
26. Barbera and McBrien, *Stevie*, 236, 239.
27. Ibid., 243

28. Hugh Gordon Porteus, "Sibyl," *Spectator* 209 (19 October 1962): 610.
29. Barbera and McBrien, *Stevie*, 245.
30. Dick, *Ivy and Stevie*, 66–67.
31. John Horder, "Poet Exposed," *Catholic Herald*, 6 January 1967, 48.
32. Barbera and McBrien, *Stevie*, 5.
33. Barbera and McBrien, *Stevie*, 295.

Chapter Two

1. Christopher Reed, "The Unbuttoned Buttonholer," *Times Literary Supplement*, 29 November 1985, 1369.
2. *Novel on Yellow Paper* (1936; reprint, London: Virago, 1980), 198; hereafter cited in the text as *NYP*
3. *Over the Frontier* (1938; reprint, London: Virago, 1980), 37; hereafter cited in the text as *OF.*
4. Barbera and McBrien, *Stevie*, 109–10.
5. *The Holiday* (1949; reprint, London: Virago, 1979), 110; hereafter cited in the text as *H.*
6. Dick, *Ivy and Stevie*, 73–74.
7. Barbera and McBrien, *Stevie*, 168.
8. Hermione Lee, "Fits & Splinters," *New Statesman*, 97 (4 May 1979): 653.

Chapter Three

1. Barbera and McBrien, *Stevie*, 137.
2. Ibid., 151.

Chapter Four

1. Seamus Heaney, "A Memorable Voice," in *Preoccupations: Selected Prose, 1968–1978* (New York: Farrar, Straus & Giroux, 1980), 199–201.
2. Anthony Thwaite, *Twentieth-Century English Poetry: An Introduction* (London; Heinemann, 1978), 86.
3. Arthur C. Rankin, *The Poetry of Stevie Smith: Little Lost Girl* (Gerrards Cross, Buckinghamshire: Colin Smythe, 1985), 15.
4. *A Good Time Was Had by All* (London: Jonathan Cape, 1937), 39; hereafter cited in the text as *GT.*
5. Calvin Bedient, "Stevie Smith," in *Eight Contemporary Poets* (London: Oxford University Press, 1974), 139.
6. Christopher Ricks, "Stevie Smith," *Grand Street* 1 (Autumn 1981): 148.
7. *Tender Only to One* (London: Jonathan Cape, 1938), 7; hereafter cited in the text as *TO.*
8. Rankin, *Poetry of Stevie Smith*, 34.
9. Porteus, "Sibyl," 610.

10. Mark Storey, "Why Stevie Smith Matters," *Critical Quarterly* 21, no. 2 (Summer 1979): 41.

11. Francis Thompson, *Poems and Essays,* ed. Wilfred Meynell (1947; reprint, Freeport, N.Y.: Books for Libraries Press, 1969), 109.

12. *Mother, What Is Man?* (London: Jonathan Cape, 1942), 45; hereafter cited in the text as *M*.

13. Patricia Meyer Spacks, *The Female Imagination* (New York: Knopf, 1975), 158.

14. Philip Larkin, "Frivolous and Vulnerable," *New Statesman* 64 (28 September 1962): 416.

Chapter Five

1. Joyce Carol Oates, "A Child with a Cold, Cold Eye," *New York Times Book Review,* 3 October 1982, 26.

2. *Harold's Leap* (London: Chapman & Hall, 1950), 15; hereafter cited in the text as *HL*.

3. "On a Broomstick," *Times Literary Supplement,* 1 December 1950, 771.

4. Michael Tatham, "That one must speak lightly . . . A study of Stevie Smith," *New Blackfriars* 53 (July 1972): 318.

5. Muriel Spark, "Melancholy Humour," *Observer* 3 (November 1957): 16.

6. *Not Waving but Drowning* (London: Deutsch, 1957), 13; hereafter cited in the text as *NW*.

7. Catherine A. Civello, "Smith's *Not Waving but Drowning,*" *Explicator* 42 (Fall 1983): 59.

8. Barbera and McBrien, *Stevie,* 204–5.

9. Janice Thaddeus, "Stevie Smith and the Gleeful Macabre," *Contemporary Poetry* 3 (1978): 46.

Chapter Six

1. *Selected Poems* (London: Longmans, Green, 1962), 1; hereafter cited in the text as *SP*.

2. *The Frog Prince and Other Poems* (London: Longmans, Green, 1966), 1; hereafter cited in the text as *FP*.

3. Sylvia Plath, "Context," *The London Magazine* 1 (February 1962): 46.

4. *The Best Beast* (New York: Knopf, 1969), 12; hereafter cited in the text as *BB*.

Chapter Seven

1. Rankin, *Poetry of Stevie Smith,* 46.

2. *Scorpion and Other Poems* (London: Longmans, Green, 1972), 1; hereafter cited in the text as *S*.

3. Barbera and McBrien, *Stevie,* 292.

4. Ibid., 292–93.
5. *The Collected Poems of Stevie Smith* (London: Allen Lane, 1975), 570; hereafter cited in the text as *CP.* "Goodnight" first appears in the 1978 edition.

Chapter Eight

1. Barbera and McBrien, *Stevie,* 299.
2. Larkin, "Frivolous and Vulnerable," 416.
3. Heaney, "A Memorable Voice," 200.
4. Bedient, "Stevie Smith," 158.
5. Spacks, *The Female Imagination,* 315.
6. Thaddeus, "Stevie Smith and the Gleeful Macabre," 48.
7. Oates, "A Child with a Cold, Cold Eye," 26.

Selected Bibliography

PRIMARY WORKS

Poetry

A Good Time Was Had by All. London: Jonathan Cape, 1937.
Tender Only to One. London: Jonathan Cape, 1938
Mother, What Is Man? London: Jonathan Cape, 1942.
Harold's Leap. London: Chapman & Hall, 1950.
Not Waving but Drowning. London: Deutsch, 1957.
Selected Poems. London: Longmans, Green, 1962; New York: New Directions, 1964.
The Frog Prince and Other Poems. London: Longmans, Green, 1966.
The Best Beast. New York: Knopf, 1969.
Scorpion and Other Poems. London: Longmans, Green, 1971.
The Collected Poems of Stevie Smith. London: Allen Lane, 1975, 1978; New
    York: Oxford University Press, 1976; New Directions, 1983; London:
    Penguin, 1985.

Novels

Novel on Yellow Paper. London: Jonathan Cape, 1936; New York: Morrow, 1937;
    Harmondsworth: Penguin, 1951, 1972; New York: Popular Library 1976;
    London: Virago, 1980; New York: Pinnacle, 1982.
Over the Frontier. London: Jonathan Cape, 1938, 1958; Virago, 1980: New York:
    Pinnacle, 1982.
The Holiday. London: Chapman & Hall, 1949; Virago, 1979; New York: Pinna-
    cle, 1982.

Other Books

Some Are More Human than Others: Sketchbook. London: Gaberbocchus, 1958.
Cats in Colour. Edited, and with an introduction by Stevie Smith. London: Batsford,
    1959; New York: Viking, 1960.
The Batsford Book of Children's Verse. Edited and with a preface by Stevie Smith.
    London: Batsford, 1970; reprinted as *The Poet's Garden,* New York: Vi-
    king, 1970.
Me Again: Uncollected Writings of Stevie Smith. Edited by Jack Barbera and William
    McBrien. London: Virago, 1981; New York: Farrar, Straus and Giroux, 1982;
    Vintage, 1983.

SECONDARY WORKS

Bibliography

Barbera, Jack, William McBrien, and Helen Bajan. *Stevie Smith: A Bibliography.* Westport, Conn.: Meckler, 1987. A thorough bibliography of all of Stevie Smith's published and unpublished work and letters, as well as all reviews and articles about her. Indispensible research tool.

Books and Articles

Barbera, Jack, and William McBrien. *Stevie: A Biography of Stevie Smith.* London: Heinemann, 1985; New York, Oxford University Press, 1987. Painstaking, exhaustive, definitive literary biography.
Bedient, Calvin. "Stevie Smith." In *Eight Contemporary Poets,* 139–58. London: Oxford University Press, 1974. Early study validates Stevie's protean talent. Explicates key poems.
Dick, Kay. *Ivy & Stevie: Ivy Compton-Burnett and Stevie Smith.* London: Duckworth, 1971; Allison & Busby, 1983. Insightful, intimate interview.
Enright, D. J. "Did Nobody Teach You? On Stevie Smith." *Encounter,* June 1971, 53–57. Reprinted in *Man Is an Onion: Reviews and Essays,* 137–48. London: Chatto, 1972. Singles out the virtues of Stevie's poetry: absence of clutter, refreshing anarchy, and high rate of success.
Heaney, Seamus. "A Memorable Voice," *Irish Times,* 3 April 1976, 8. Reprinted in *Preoccupations: Selected Prose, 1968–1978,* 199–201. London: Faber, 1980. Sees Stevie presenting a world reflected in a wobbly mirror.
Lawson, Elizabeth. "Stevie Smith and Metaphors of Disengagement." *Sydney Studies in English* 9 (1983–84): 94–106. A study of the "deathwardness" of Stevie's poetry.
Oates, Joyce Carol. "A Child with a Cold, Cold Eye." *New York Times Book Review,* 3 October 1982, pp. 11, 26. A retrospective on Stevie's novels, considering her work an "acquired taste."
Pumphrey, Martin. "Play, Fantasy and Strange Laughter: Stevie Smith's Uncomfortable Poetry." *Critical Quarterly* 28, no. 3 (Autumn 1986): 85–96. The role of fantasy, play, and "childishness" in Stevie's poetry.
Rankin, Arthur C. *The Poetry of Stevie Smith: Little Lost Girl.* Gerrards Cross, Buckinghamshire: Colin Smythe, 1985. Excellent thematic study of Stevie's poetry emphasizing religious values and the spiritual itinerary of the canon.
Ricks, Christopher. "Stevie Smith." *Grand Street* 1 (Autumn 1981): 147–157. Revised and reprinted as "Stevie Smith: The Art of Sinking in Poetry." In *The Force of Poetry,* 244–55. Oxford: Clarendon Press, 1984. Finds Stevie's use of fooling, clichés, and mock criticism to be profound. Compares Stevie to Samuel Beckett.

Spalding, Frances. *Stevie Smith.* London: Faber 1988; New York: W.W. Norton, 1989. The authorized biography. Concentrates on the relationship between Stevie's life and her work. Adds little to Barbera and McBrien.

Storey, Mark. "Why Stevie Smith Matters." *Critical Quarterly* 21, no. 2 (Summer 1979): 41–55. The uniqueness of Stevie's poetry is in the way it comes to terms with death.

Tatham, Michael. "That One Must Speak Lightly . . . A Study of Stevie Smith." *New Blackfriars* 53 (July 1972): 318–27. Stevie Smith as major religious poet.

Thaddeus, Janice. "Stevie Smith and the Gleeful Macabre." *Contemporary Poetry* 3 (1978): 36–49. Commitment and rejection, sadness and desperation, the child and the adult in Stevie's poetry.

Wade, Stephen. "Stevie Smith and the Untruth of Myth." *Agenda* 15 (Summer–Autumn 1977): 102–6. Argues that Stevie wants myth to be considered, like religion, a unit of personal significance.

Williams, Jonathan. "Much Further Out than You Thought." *Parnassus: Poetry in Review* 2 (Spring–Summer 1974): 105–27. Interview conducted 13 September 1963. A celebration of Stevie's poetry and prose.

Index